Moorabye County Library
Super modern library
DISCARDED

641.8
SWE

D0604129

JUN 0 8 2011

SPECIAL
cupcakes

SPECIAL
cupcakes

WENDY SWEETSER

NEW HOLLAND

First published in 2011 by New Holland Publishers (UK) Ltd
London • Cape Town • Sydney • Auckland

Garfield House
86–88 Edgware Rd
London W2 2EA
United Kingdom

Unit 1
66 Gibbes Street
Chatswood, NSW 2067
Australia

80 McKenzie Street
Cape Town 8001
South Africa

218 Lake Road
Northcote, Auckland
New Zealand

Text copyright © 2011 Wendy Sweetser
Copyright © 2011 New Holland Publishers (UK) Ltd

Wendy Sweetser has asserted her moral right to be identified
as the author of this work.

All rights reserved. No part of this publication may be
reproduced, stored in a retrieval system, or transmitted
in any form or by any means, electronic, mechanical,
photocopying, recording or otherwise, without the prior
written permission of the publishers and copyright holders.

ISBN   978 1 84773 855 4

Publisher: **Clare Sayer**
Senior Editor: **Emma Pattison**
Designer: **Lucy Parissi**
Photography: **Ian Garlick**
Food Stylist: **Wendy Sweetser**
Production: **Laurence Poos**

1 3 5 7 9 10 8 6 4 2

Reproduction by Pica Digital PTE Ltd, Singapore
Printed and bound in Malaysia by Times Offset
(M) Sdn Bhd

Contents

Introduction

Sex and the City's Carrie and Miranda might have introduced cupcakes to millions of new fans as they agonized over Carrie's new love Aiden at the Magnolia Bakery in New York City's West Village, but these dainty little cakes have in fact been around for much longer. As far back as 1796 Amelia Simmons was talking about 'cakes baked in small cups' in her *American Cookery* book and just over 30 years later in 1828 the first mention of a 'cupcake' can be found in Eliza Leslie's *Receipts*. However, it wasn't until after the First World War that small, individual cakes packed in boxes for easy transportation became widely available and a hit with the public. Two theories have emerged as to how these 'single person' cakes came to be known as cupcakes. The first suggests it was the method of measuring the ingredients in cups, the second that the cakes themselves were baked in cups. Whichever is correct there is certainly no disputing their popularity today.

All the recipes in this book are easy to follow and don't need any special baking skills to create them. As well as cupcakes for special occasions that can be decorated as simply or as elaborately as the mood takes you, I've included recipes for those drab days when you need a treat to cheer you up, giant cupcakes to wow your friends, and I've not forgotten the people on restricted diets who normally have to decline when cakes are being passed around. I've created recipes that I hope will appeal to all ages too, with simple ideas for children and more sophisticated combinations of textures and flavours for grown ups.

And, of course, if you fancy combining the cake mixture from one recipe with the frosting from another, you can mix and match as much as you like – when it comes to cupcakes the possibilities are endless and the choice is yours!

Equipment

THE BASICS

As with all cake making you'll need scales, measuring jug and spoons, a mixing bowl, wooden spoons, a manual or electric hand whisk, grater and cooling rack. Other equipment such as a liquidizer or food processor will be useful for some recipes but not essential.

MUFFIN AND BUN TRAYS

When baking cupcakes in paper cases, put the cases in muffin or bun trays so the cakes keep their shape during baking. If you don't want to use paper cases, the cake mixture can be spooned straight into the cups of the tray as long as they are greased first to ensure the cupcakes can be removed easily. Non-stick or silicone moulds or trays don't need to be greased as the cupcakes will simply pop out.

PAPER CASES

Any keen cupcake maker will soon discover that paper cases come in an alarming number of different sizes with the majority of recipes saying 'makes 12' with no indication as to the size of cases used. The majority of the cupcakes in this book are baked in standard muffin cases (see below) but where I've used a different size this is indicated. Cases have the following measurements:

Mini – base 2.5 cm (1 in), height 2.5 cm (1 in)
Small – base 4 cm (1½ in), height 2.5 cm (1 in)
Fairy cake – base 5 cm (2 in), height 2.5 cm (1 in)
Medium – base 5 cm (2 in), height 3 cm (1¼ in)
Standard – base 6 cm (2½ in), height 4 cm (1½ in)

You can of course substitute different sizes of cases from the ones I've used, it just means you'll make more or fewer cupcakes and cooking times will need to be adjusted.

Making cupcakes

BASIC CUPCAKE RECIPE

Although I've created lots of different cupcake mixes for the recipes in this book, basic cupcakes can be made from a classic sponge mix in the following way:

1 Put 175 g (6 oz) butter in a mixing bowl and beat until smooth. Gradually beat in 175 g (6 oz) sugar until light and creamy. I recommend using unsalted butter and this needs to be soft so it is easier to beat with the sugar. If you've forgotten to take the block of butter out of the fridge in advance and it's rock hard, cut the measured quantity into small pieces and microwave it in the mixing bowl for 1 minute on defrost to bring it to the required softness. Caster, golden caster and light and dark brown muscovado sugars can all be used. The sugars given in the recipes can be substituted with others if you prefer.

2 Beat 3 large eggs together and gradually add them to the creamed mixture, beating well after each addition. If the mixture curdles before all the egg has been added, stir in a little of the measured quantity of flour. If you only have medium or small eggs to hand, these can be used but you may need to add a little extra milk or fruit juice at the end of the recipe to bring the batter to the required consistency.

3 Mix in 175 g (6 oz) self-raising flour and 2 tablespoons of milk or fruit juice, stirring well until all the ingredients are combined and you have a soft mixture that drops off the spoon when lifted.

4 Spoon the cake mixture into a muffin tray lined with 12 paper cases, filling the cases about two-thirds full. Bake in the oven at 180C/350F/Gas mark 4 for 15-20 minutes until golden brown and risen.

5 Leave the cupcakes in the tray for 10 minutes before lifting them out on to a wire rack to cool completely.

TESTING TO SEE IF YOUR CUPCAKES ARE COOKED

Light sponge mixtures, such as the basic recipe opposite, can be tested for 'doneness' by pressing the top of a cake gently – it should spring back. Heavier mixtures are best tested by pushing a skewer into the centre of one of the cakes and it should come out clean. Heavier mixtures also rise less so the paper cases can be three-quarters filled.

ADDING FRUIT AND OTHER FLAVOURINGS

Grated citrus rind, sweet spices such as cinnamon and ginger, nuts, cocoa, desiccated coconut and flavouring essences such as vanilla, almond or coffee can all be added to the basic cake mix. Fresh fruit can be mixed into the batter but chop any large fruit into small pieces and dust the fruit with some of the measured flour before stirring in to prevent it sinking to the bottom during baking.

COLOURING CUPCAKES

Food colourings can be used but other ingredients such as liqueurs and syrups can be added as well. Try crème de menthe for green, grenadine syrup for pink, blue Curaçao for blue, chocolate or coffee essence for brown and toffee sauce for caramel. If using bought food colourings, add them sparingly as they are very strong and not everyone finds fluorescent icing attractive!

ICING CUPCAKES

The individual recipes in this book have their own suggested frostings and icings but these can be swopped between recipes or you can add extra ingredients to suit your personal taste.

To frost a cupcake with buttercream, hold the cake by the base and top with a spoonful of frosting in the centre. Gradually spread this over the cake in a circular movement using a small palette knife or other round-bladed knife until the top is covered almost to the edge of the paper case. Butter cream frosting can also be piped over a cupcake. Spoon the frosting into a piping bag fitted with a large star nozzle and pipe in concentric circles over the top of the cakes, starting in the centre. If you pipe frosting you'll probably find you use more, as piped toppings tend to be thicker than those that have been spread on with a knife. To ice a cupcake with glacé icing, sieve icing sugar into a bowl and stir in just enough water or another liquid to make a thick, spreadable icing. Spoon it on top of the cupcakes and spread almost to the edge of the paper case with a knife or let the icing run down and find its own level.

EXTRAS TO MAKE YOUR CUPCAKES SPECIAL

One of the simplest ways to decorate a frosted cupcake is to put some granulated or caster sugar in a small plastic bag, add a little powdered food colouring, seal the bag and shake it vigorously. The coloured sugar can then be sprinkled over the frosting. Tubs of ready-made sugar sprinkles are also available in a rainbow of colours from larger supermarkets and websites. For more eye-catching decorations, you can either make your own novelties or buy ready-made ones from cook shop or websites advertising 'equipment for making cupcakes' that can be purchased by mail order. Flowers, fruits, Christmas decorations, Easter chicks and wedding novelties can be moulded from coloured sugarpaste icing or marzipan with details added using coloured writing icings.

DRESS UP A CUPCAKE

Bored with plain cupcakes? Why not bake the cakes in silicone moulds without paper cases and spread the sides with buttercream before rolling in chopped nuts, toasted desiccated coconut or crumbled chocolate flake? Or split cupcakes horizontally in half and sandwich with buttercream or whipped cream and fresh fruit, or wrap a chocolate collar around. To do this, measure the circumference and height of a cupcake by wrapping a piece of baking parchment around the cake and drawing a rectangle on the parchment showing how large the collar needs to be. Melt chocolate, spoon into a greaseproof paper piping bag and snip off the end. Pipe over the outline of the rectangle and leave to set before spooning in enough melted chocolate to fill the rectangle. Leave until no longer runny but not set. Spread the sides of the cupcake with buttercream and wrap the chocolate collar around the cake, leaving it to set firmly before peeling away the parchment.

GIVE YOUR CUPCAKES AS GIFTS

If you're giving your cupcakes to a friend as a special gift, decorated boxes with see-through lids and cellophane bags tied with ribbons are attractive ways of packaging them. Boxes and bags can be bought from cook shops and websites.

NOTES ON THE RECIPES

• The quantities of frostings given for the individual recipes allow for an average layer to be spread over the tops of the cupcakes.

• Preparation times given are for making the cupcake mixture and coating with icing or frosting once the cakes have cooled. Extra time needs to be added for making special decorations.

• As ovens vary, the recipe cooking times should only be taken as a guide. If you're new to cupcake baking, keep an eye on your cakes towards the end of cooking to ensure they don't overcook and test carefully to see if they're done.

• Most recipes for larger cakes can be adapted for cupcakes if you have a favourite mix. The same quantity of mixture needed to make a 20.5 cm (8 in) round cake will make 12 cupcakes using standard paper cases, just reduce the cooking time to around 20 minutes in a 180°C/350°F/gas mark 4 oven.

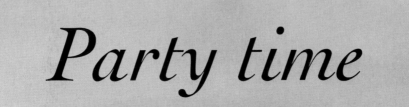

Party time

Banana and salt caramel

These will do down really well at teenagers' birthday parties. How much salt you add to the frosting is very much down to personal taste, which is why it's preferable to make it with unsalted butter rather than salted and add the salt separately. Salt caramels originate from Brittany where sweet makers prized the local *sel de Guérande* from the Ile de Ré so much they added it to their soft, creamy caramels.

Preparation time: 30 minutes (plus cooling and chilling)
Cooking time: 20 minutes
Makes: 20 (using medium-size cases)

Banana cupcakes

140 g (5 oz) unsalted butter, melted and cooled
200 g (7 oz) light muscovado sugar
2 large eggs, beaten
3 small ripe bananas, peeled and chopped (about 350 g / 12 oz unpeeled weight)
1 tsp ground cinnamon
4 tbsp natural yoghurt
300 g (11 oz) plain flour
½ tsp baking powder
1 tsp bicarbonate of soda
50 g (2 oz) chopped pecans

Salt caramel frosting

175 g (6 oz) granulated sugar
175 ml (6 fl oz) double cream
1 tsp vanilla extract
½ tsp sea salt (or more to taste)
140 g (5 oz) unsalted butter

To decorate

Chocolate salt caramel buttons, popcorn and chocolate vermicelli

1 First make the cupcakes. Preheat the oven to 180°C/350°F/gas mark 4. Line muffin trays with 20 paper cases.

2 Put the melted butter, muscovado sugar, eggs, bananas, cinnamon and yoghurt in a liquidizer or food processor and blend until smooth. Sieve together the flour, baking powder and bicarbonate of soda into a mixing bowl and pour in the liquidized mixture. Stir or whisk until combined, add the pecans and mix in.

3 Spoon into the paper cases and bake for 20 minutes or until golden brown and a skewer pushed into the centre of a cake comes out clean. Cool in the tin for 10 minutes before transferring to a wire rack to cool completely.

4 To make the frosting put the granulated sugar in a pan, add 2 tablespoons water and heat gently until the sugar dissolves. Bring to the boil and bubble until the syrup caramelises to a dark amber colour. Remove from the heat and gradually beat in the cream, vanilla and sea salt with a wooden spoon. Set aside to cool for 30 minutes.

5 In a bowl, beat the butter until creamy and then beat in the caramel mixture a little at a time. Cool completely and then chill to firm up, stirring occasionally.

6 Spread or pipe the frosting over the cupcakes and decorate with chocolate salt caramels buttons, popcorn and vermicelli.

Tip

If you add the cream too quickly and the caramel sets in hard lumps, microwave on medium power to re-melt, stirring every 30 seconds.

Rocky road

These no-bake treats will have children and adults alike coming back for more. You can stir whatever combination of nuts and dried fruits you like into the melted chocolate, an ideal way of using up those half empty packets taking up space in the kitchen cupboard. As these are quite rich, it's best to make them in fairy cake cases rather than larger muffin cases.

Preparation time: 20 minutes
(plus setting)
Makes: 18 (using fairy cake cases)

Rocky road treats

115 g (4 oz) plain chocolate

1 tbsp golden syrup

115 g (4 oz) unsalted butter

2 tbsp thick natural yoghurt

12 digestive biscuits, broken
into small pieces

115 g (4 oz) mini marshmallows

75 g (3 oz) no-soak dried apricots,
chopped

50 g (2 oz) pecans, coarsely chopped

To decorate

50 g (2 oz) dark or milk chocolate

1 Line bun-trays with 18 fairy cake paper cases.

2 Put the plain chocolate, golden syrup and butter in a pan large enough to take all the ingredients and heat very gently until melted, stirring occasionally until smooth. Remove from the heat and stir in the yoghurt.

3 Add the biscuits, three-quarters of the marshmallows, the apricots and pecans to the chocolate mixture and stir until everything is well coated.

4 Spoon the mixture into the paper cases, pushing down with the back of the spoon. Press the remaining marshmallows on top and leave in a cool place until set.

5 To decorate, melt the dark or milk chocolate and drizzle or pipe over the top of the cupcakes and leave to set again.

Niobrara County Library
Lusk, Wyoming 82225

 *Tip*

If preferred, use shortbread biscuits, ginger nuts or another plain biscuit instead of digestives.

17

Independence Day cranberry and maple

Although these cupcakes have an American theme they can be adapted for other national celebrations such as Bastille Day, St George's Day or Anzac Day by changing the colour and style of the decorations to fit the national flag.

Preparation time: 30 minutes (plus cooling)

Cooking time: 20–25 minutes

Makes: 12

Cranberry cupcakes

175 g (6 oz) unsalted butter, softened

140 g (5 oz) caster sugar

3 tbsp maple syrup

3 large eggs, beaten

225 g (8 oz) self-raising flour

75 g (3 oz) dried cranberries

2 tbsp cranberry juice

Vanilla frosting

1½ tbsp maple syrup

40 g (1½ oz) unsalted butter, cut into small pieces

2 tsp milk

175 g (6 oz) icing sugar

½ tsp vanilla extract

Red and blue sugarpaste icing, to decorate

1 To make the cupcakes, preheat the oven to 180°C/350°F/gas mark 4. Line a 12-cup muffin tray with paper cases.

2 Beat the butter and caster sugar together until smooth and then stir in the maple syrup. Mix in the eggs, a little at a time, fold in the flour and finally add the cranberries and cranberry juice, stirring until just combined with the other ingredients.

3 Spoon the mixture into the paper cases and bake for 20–25 minutes until golden brown and springy to the touch. Cool in the tin for 10 minutes before removing to a wire rack to cool completely.

4 To make the frosting, put the maple syrup, butter and milk in a small bowl and microwave on full power for 1 minute or until the butter has melted. Sieve the icing sugar into a mixing bowl, add the vanilla to the melted mixture and pour it on to the icing sugar, stirring until smooth. Allow to cool, then beat with a wooden spoon until thick.

5 Spread the icing over the cupcakes and decorate with stars and stripes cut from rolled out red and blue sugarpaste icing.

 *Tip*

If making the cupcakes when cranberries are in season, fresh cranberries can be used but microwave or cook them in a pan over a gentle heat for a couple of minutes first until the berries pop and soften.

Halloween pumpkin and ginger

A sweet treat for trick or treaters made all the more fun by adding spooky decorations such as witches' hats, pumpkins and spiders. The undecorated cupcakes can be made ahead and frozen, whilst the novelty decorations can also be prepared in advance and stored in a cool, dry place.

Preparation time: 30 minutes (plus cooling and making decorations)

Cooking time: 15–20 minutes

Makes: 12

Pumpkin cupcakes

225 g (8 oz) self-raising flour

1½ tsp bicarbonate of soda

2 tsp ground ginger

200 g (7 oz) light muscovado sugar

125 g (4½ oz) raisins

140 g (5 oz) unsalted butter, melted and cooled

3 large eggs

Finely grated rind of 1 small orange

1 tbsp orange juice

200 g (7 oz) raw pumpkin flesh, grated

To decorate

4 tbsp apricot jam or orange marmalade, sieved

175 g (6 oz) each orange and black sugarpaste icing or coloured marzipan, plus small amounts of green and white for pumpkins and witches' hats

Coloured writing icing

1 To make the cupcakes, preheat the oven to 180°C/350°F/gas mark 4 and line a 12-cup muffin tray with paper cases.

2 Sieve the flour, bicarbonate of soda and ginger into a large jug or mixing bowl and stir in the sugar and raisins. Beat together the melted butter, eggs, orange rind and juice and pour into the dry ingredients, mixing until evenly combined. Stir in the grated pumpkin.

3 Spoon the mixture into the paper cases and bake for 15–20 minutes until golden brown and a skewer pressed into the centre of a cake comes out clean. Cool in the tin for 10 minutes before removing to a wire rack to cool completely.

4 To decorate, warm the sieved jam or marmalade and brush over the tops of the cupcakes. Cover with thinly rolled orange or black sugarpaste icing or marzipan, pressing down lightly in an even layer and trimming the edges.

5 Gather up trimmings from the icing or marzipan and mould into tiny pumpkins, spiders or witches' hats. Fix in place on top of the cupcakes with a little writing icing. Decorate some cupcakes with piped cobwebs.

 Tip

Grated squash can replace the pumpkin if you prefer. The quantity given is for the flesh after it has been peeled and deseeded.

Blueberry and white chocolate

Tangy blueberries, light sponge and a creamy chocolate icing make these summer cupcakes just right for a summer party or picnic. If transporting them in warm weather, keep the cupcakes cool in a chiller box or bag so the icing doesn't soften too much.

Preparation time: 30 minutes
(plus cooling and setting)
Cooking time: 15 minutes
Makes: 12

Blueberry cupcakes

140g (5oz) unsalted butter, softened
140g (5oz) caster sugar
Finely grated zest of 1 small lemon
4 large egg whites
115 g (4 oz) blueberries
75 g (3 oz) plain flour
115 g (4 oz) ground almonds

White chocolate icing

175 g (6 oz) white chocolate, chopped
4 tbsp double cream
Extra grated or shaved white chocolate and blueberries, to decorate

1 To make the cupcakes, preheat the oven to 180°C/350°F/gas mark 4. Line a 12-cup muffin tray with paper cases.

2 Beat the butter and caster sugar together until creamy. Beat in the lemon zest. In a separate bowl, whisk the egg whites until standing in soft peaks. Dust the blueberries with a little of the flour.

3 Stir the blueberries into the creamed mixture with the rest of the flour and the almonds. Mix in a spoonful of the whisked egg whites to soften the mixture before gently folding in the rest with a large metal spoon.

4 Spoon the mixture into the paper cases and bake for 15 minutes or until golden and just firm to the touch. Cool in the tin for 10 minutes before removing to a wire rack to cool completely.

5 To make the icing, put the chocolate and cream in a heatproof bowl and place over a pan of simmering water. Leave until the chocolate has melted, stirring until smooth. Remove the bowl from the pan and set aside in a cool place until the icing has thickened sufficiently to spread over the cupcakes, stirring from time to time.

6 Ice the cupcakes and decorate with grated white chocolate and blueberries.

Seasonal celebrations

Festive spice with brandy cream

A rich fruitcake that is packed with sweet spices and dried fruits might be a Christmas tradition in many countries but there are plenty of us who prefer something less heavy after all the feasting. These cupcakes make the perfect alternative – light and melt-in-the-mouth with the aroma of cinnamon, nutmeg and ginger and a creamy brandy frosting to keep out the cold.

Preparation time: 30 minutes
(plus cooling and chilling)
Cooking time: 20-25 minutes
Makes: 12

Spiced cupcakes

175 g (6 oz) unsalted butter, softened
175 g (6 oz) golden caster sugar
3 large eggs, separated
175 g (6 oz) self-raising flour
1 tsp ground cinnamon
1 tsp ground ginger
Pinch of ground nutmeg
50 g (2 oz) ground almonds
1 tbsp milk

Brandy frosting

75 g (3 oz) unsalted butter, softened
115 g (4 oz) golden icing sugar, sieved
2 tbsp brandy
Marzipan fruits, to decorate

1 To make the cupcakes, preheat the oven to 180°C/350°F/gas mark 4. Line a 12-cup muffin tray with paper cases.

2 Beat the butter in a bowl until creamy and then gradually beat in the sugar until light. Beat in the egg yolks, one at a time, and then stir in the flour, cinnamon, ginger, nutmeg, almonds and milk.

3 Whisk the egg whites until standing in soft peaks. Stir one tablespoon into the mixture to soften it before carefully folding in the rest until evenly combined.

4 Transfer the mixture to a large jug and carefully pour it into the paper cases. Bake for 20–25 minutes until golden brown and risen. Cool in the tin for 10 minutes before transferring the cupcakes to a wire rack to cool completely.

5 To make the frosting, beat the butter until creamy, then gradually beat in the icing sugar. Finally beat in the brandy a few drops at a time. Chill in the fridge for 1–2 hours to firm up.

6 Spread the frosting over the cupcakes and decorate with small marzipan fruits, bought or homemade.

 Tip

When beating the brandy into the frosting, only add a very little at a time or the mixture will curdle.

Brazil nut and clementine

Tiny, sweet clementines with their loose, easy-peel skins are always a favourite with children and they add a tangy fruity flavour to these cupcakes. Larger supermarkets and cake decorating equipment suppliers sell Christmas novelties that can be used to decorate the cakes or you can have fun getting all the family to help you make your own.

Preparation time: 25 minutes
(plus cooling and decorating)
Cooking time: 15–20 minutes
Makes: 15

Cupcakes

175 g (6 oz) unsalted butter, softened
175 g (6 oz) caster sugar
3 large eggs, beaten
1–2 clementines, depending on size
175 g (6 oz) self-raising flour
75 g (3 oz) Brazil nuts, finely chopped

Clementine glacé icing

3–4 tbsp clementine juice
275 g (10 oz) icing sugar, sieved

To decorate

Edible white glitter
Christmas novelties made from coloured marzipan or sugarpaste icing and coloured writing icing

1 To make the cupcakes, preheat the oven to 180°C/350°F/gas mark 4. Line muffin trays with 15 paper cases.

2 In a mixing bowl, beat the butter and caster sugar together until soft and creamy. Gradually beat in the eggs. Peel the clementines, pulling off any loose strands of pith, and chop them into small pieces. Dust with a little of the flour until coated.

3 Stir the remaining flour and clementine pieces into the creamed mixture until evenly combined.

4 Spoon the mixture into the paper cases and bake for 15–20 minutes or until springy to the touch. Cool in the trays for 10 minutes before removing to a wire rack to cool completely.

5 To make the icing, stir enough clementine juice into the icing sugar to make a smooth, spreadable icing. Spread over the cupcakes, sprinkle with edible white glitter to resemble snow and add Christmas novelties such as Santas, snowmen, Rudolf the red-nosed reindeer or Christmas trees.

 Tip

To make the Christmas figures, roll out coloured marzipan or sugarpaste icing thinly on a surface dusted with icing sugar and cut out shapes using a small sharp knife. Assemble the figures by dampening the underside of the shapes with a little water and pressing them in place. Finish with coloured writing icing.

Chocolate and physalis

Christmas wouldn't be Christmas without some chocolatey treats and these rich, velvety cupcakes certainly fit the bill. Physalis, also known as Cape gooseberries, make a pretty decoration with their Chinese paper lantern wrappers carefully opened and pushed back.

Preparation time: 30 minutes
(plus cooling)
Cooking time: 20 minutes
Makes: 18 (using medium-sized cases)

Chocolate cupcakes

2 tsp lemon juice
175 ml (6 fl oz) milk
175 g (6 oz) plain flour
1 tsp bicarbonate of soda
50 g (2 oz) cocoa powder
75 g (3 oz) unsalted butter, softened
175 g (6 oz) dark muscovado sugar
2 large eggs, beaten
6 physalis

Chocolate frosting

200 g (7 oz) dark chocolate
150 ml (¼ pt) full fat soured cream
18 physalis

1 To make the cupcakes, preheat the oven to 180°C/350°F/gas mark 4 and line muffin or bun trays with 18 medium-sized paper cases.

2 Stir the lemon juice into the milk and set aside. Sieve the flour, bicarbonate of soda and cocoa powder together.

3 In a mixing bowl, beat the butter until creamy and then gradually beat in the muscovado sugar. Beat in the eggs a little at a time and then fold in the flour mixture alternately with the milk. Remove physalis from their paper-like wrappers, chop and stir in.

4 Spoon the mixture into the paper cases and bake in the oven for 20 minutes or until a skewer pushed into the centre of a cake comes out clean. Cool in the tray for 10 minutes before transferring to a wire rack to cool completely.

5 To make the frosting, chop 175 g (6 oz) of the chocolate, place in a bowl over a pan of simmering water. Leave until melted, stirring occasionally until smooth. Stir in the soured cream and chill, if necessary, until firm enough to spread over the tops of the cupcakes. If you chill the frosting for too long and it becomes too thick, microwave it for 1 minute on low power to soften, stirring well before using.

6 Grate the remaining chocolate and sprinkle over the cupcakes. Decorate each with a whole physalis with its papery covering folded back.

Cupcake Christmas tree

This edible 'tree' will make a striking centrepiece for a Christmas buffet table, especially if you can track down a stand that has a star on top – if not, you can always add your own to a plain stand. The undecorated cupcakes can be made up to 8 weeks ahead and frozen until needed.

Preparation time: 25 minutes
(plus cooling and decorating)
Cooking time: 12–15 minutes
Makes: 24 (using fairy cake cases)

Cashew cupcakes

175 g (6 oz) unsalted butter, softened
75 g (3 oz) golden caster sugar
75 g (3 oz) light muscovado sugar
Grated rind of 1 lemon
3 large eggs, beaten
225 g (8 oz) self-raising flour
50 g (2 oz) cashews, finely chopped

Lemon frosting

140 g (5 oz) unsalted butter, softened
250 g (9 oz) icing sugar, sieved
2–3 tbsp lemon juice
Green food colouring

To decorate

Christmas motifs, such as holly, parcels, mistletoe, candles or crackers, made from coloured marzipan or sugarpaste icing and coloured writing icing
Multi-coloured sugar sprinkles

1 To make the cupcakes, preheat the oven to 180°C/350°F/gas mark 4. Line two 12-cup bun trays with paper fairy cake cases.

2 Beat the butter, golden caster sugar, light muscovado sugar and lemon rind together until creamy. Gradually beat in the eggs, stir in the flour and finally the cashews until evenly combined.

3 Spoon into the paper cases and bake for 12–15 minutes until risen and springy to the touch. Cool in the trays for 10 minutes before removing the cupcakes to a wire rack to cool completely.

4 To make the frosting, beat the butter until smooth, then gradually beat in the icing sugar and lemon juice to make a soft, spreadable icing. Tint green by beating in a little food colouring.

5 Spread the frosting over the cupcakes and top with Christmas motifs modelled from coloured marzipan or sugarpaste icing and decorated with coloured writing icing. Scatter over sugar sprinkles.

Niobrara County Library
Lusk, Wyoming 82225

 Tip

If you're short of time, look for small edible Christmas decorations in larger supermarkets and use these to decorate the cupcakes.

Vanilla, poppy seed and lemon

Perfect for teatime or as a treat after the ritual Easter egg hunt, these fun cupcakes will delight all the family. Decorated with tiny Easter eggs and bought or homemade chicks tucked into crumbled chocolate flake nests, they'll disappear like magic.

Preparation time: 20 minutes
(plus cooling)
Cooking time: 20 minutes
Makes: 12

Poppy seed cupcakes

175 g (6 oz) unsalted butter, softened

175 g (6 oz) caster sugar

3 large eggs

1 tsp vanilla essence

175 g (6 oz) self-raising flour

25 g (1 oz) poppy seeds

Lemon icing

250 g (9 oz) icing sugar

1½ tbsp lemon juice

1 tsp finely grated lemon rind

To decorate

Small Easter eggs and chicks in nests made from coloured marzipan and crumbled chocolate flake

1 To make the cupcakes, preheat the oven to 180°C/350°F/gas mark 4. Line a 12-cup muffin tray with paper cases.

2 Beat the butter and caster sugar together until creamy. Beat the eggs and vanilla together and add a little at a time to the creamed mixture, beating well after each addition. Finally stir in the flour and poppy seeds.

3 Spoon the mixture into the paper cases and bake for about 20 minutes or until golden brown and springy to the touch. Cool in the tins for 10 minutes before removing to a wire rack to cool completely.

4 To make the icing, sieve the icing sugar into a bowl and stir in the lemon juice to give a smooth, spreadable icing. Stir in the lemon rind and spread the icing over the cupcakes. Decorate with small Easter eggs and chicks in nests, bought or homemade.

 Tip

Vanilla extract is the most concentrated form of flavouring, being stronger than vanilla essence, so if you prefer to use this to flavour the cupcake mixture, reduce the quantity to ½ teaspoon.

Romance

Wickedly dark chocolate and chilli

Spice things up next Valentine's Day with these wickedly rich cupcakes made from the darkest, bitterest chocolate and spiked with fiery red chilli. As fresh chillies vary so much in size and firepower, be guided by how hot you and your loved one want the evening to be!

Preparation time: 30 minutes
(plus cooling and decorating)
Cooking time: 20 minutes
Makes: 12

Chilli cupcakes

175 g (6 oz) unsalted butter, softened
140 g (5 oz) dark muscovado sugar
2 large eggs, beaten
2 tbsp golden syrup
225 g (8 oz) self-raising flour
115 g (4 oz) dark chocolate, melted
1–2 red chillies, deseeded and very finely chopped

Chocolate frosting

175 g (6 oz) best quality dark chocolate with cocoa solids of 70% or above
2 tbsp dark muscovado sugar
150 ml (¼ pt) soured cream

To decorate

Red and green coloured marzipan or sugarpaste icing moulded into chillies, luscious lips and devil's horns
Red sugar sprinkles

1 To make the cupcakes, preheat the oven to 180°C/350°F/gas mark 4. Line a 12-cup muffin tray with paper cases.

2 Beat the butter and sugar together until creamy. Gradually beat in the eggs and then stir in the golden syrup, flour, melted chocolate and chillies.

3 Spoon the mixture into the cases and bake for 20 minutes or until just firm to the touch. Cool in the tin for 10 minutes before removing to a wire rack to cool completely.

4 To make the frosting, chop or break the chocolate into small pieces and melt in a bowl placed over a pan of steaming water, stirring until smooth. Remove the bowl to the work surface and beat in the sugar until dissolved, followed by the soured cream.

5 Spread the frosting over the cupcakes and decorate with chillies, lips and devil's horns moulded from coloured marzipan or sugarpaste icing. Scatter over red sugar sprinkles.

 **Tip**

For decoration you could even use real chillies but remember, the smaller the chilli the hotter it will be.

I love you

Almond and white chocolate kisses

If dark chocolate and chillies are not your thing, these pretty cupcakes would make the perfect Valentine's Day alternative. Piled on to a tiered stand and decorated with a selection of different fruits or flowers, they would also make an eye-catching wedding cake.

Preparation time: 25 minutes (plus cooling)
Cooking time: 20 minutes
Makes: 15 (using medium-size cases)

Almond cupcakes

225 g (8 oz) self-raising flour
1 tsp baking powder
175 g (6 oz) caster sugar
3 large eggs
140 g (5 oz) natural yoghurt
50 g (2 oz) ground almonds
140 g (5 oz) unsalted butter, melted and cooled

White chocolate buttercream

75 g (3 oz) unsalted butter, softened
175 g (6 oz) icing sugar, plus extra for dusting
2 tbsp milk
75 g (3 oz) white chocolate, melted
Small sprigs of redcurrants, to decorate

1 To make the cupcakes, preheat the oven to 190°C/375°F/gas mark 5. Line muffin trays with 15 paper cases.

2 Sieve the flour and baking powder into a bowl and stir in the sugar. Whisk together the eggs, yoghurt, ground almonds and melted butter and stir into the dry ingredients until evenly combined.

3 Spoon into the paper cases and bake for 20 minutes or until golden brown and just firm to the touch. Cool in the tin for 10 minutes before removing to a wire rack to cool completely.

4 To make the buttercream, beat the butter until creamy. Gradually beat in the icing sugar until smooth and then stir in the milk and melted chocolate.

5 Cut a heart-shaped section from the top of each cupcake, using a cutter or small, sharp knife. Pipe or spoon in the buttercream and replace the hearts. Decorate each with a small sprig of redcurrants and dust with icing sugar.

 Tip

Take special care when melting white chocolate as it can quickly take on a granular texture and spoil. Break or chop the chocolate into small pieces and place it in a bowl over a pan of steaming (not boiling) water, making sure the bottom of the bowl sits above the water level. Leave until the chocolate has melted and then stir until smooth.

Orange flower engagement cupcakes

If orange curd is unavailable, make the buttercream frosting with lemon curd to add an extra citrus tang. You can be as creative as you like when decorating the cupcakes – hearts, champagne glasses or the initials of the happy couple should all produce gasps of delight when you produce them.

Preparation time: 25 minutes
(plus cooling)
Cooking time: 20 minutes
Makes: 12

Orange cupcakes

175 g (6 oz) unsalted butter, softened
175 g (6 oz) golden caster sugar
Grated rind of 1 orange
3 large eggs, beaten
175 g (6 oz) self-raising flour
1 tbsp orange flower water

Orange curd buttercream

115 g (4 oz) unsalted butter, softened
225 g (8 oz) icing sugar
2 tbsp orange curd
A little orange food colouring (optional)

To decorate

Orange sugar sprinkles

1 To make the cupcakes, preheat the oven to 180°C/350°F/gas mark 4. Line a 12-cup muffin tray with paper cases.

2 Beat the butter, caster sugar and orange rind together until creamy. Gradually beat in the eggs and then stir in the flour and orange flower water until evenly combined.

3 Spoon the mixture into the paper cases and bake for 20 minutes or until golden brown and springy to the touch. Cool in the tray for 10 minutes before removing to a wire rack to cool completely.

4 To make the buttercream, beat the butter until creamy. Gradually sieve in the icing sugar, beating well after each addition. Stir in the orange curd and tint the frosting with a few drops of orange food colouring if wished.

5 Spread the buttercream over the cupcakes and decorate with orange sprinkles. Pipe on motifs, initials or other designs using black writing icing for a final, personal flourish.

 Tip

Orange flower water – or orange blossom water as it is also called – is made by steeping bitter orange blossoms in water and then distilling the scented liquid. Available from larger supermarkets, it is a popular ingredient in North African and Mediterranean dishes.

Strawberry and soured cream

These little delights are perfect for a hen party. Although there's nothing quite so luscious as a sweet, ripe strawberry, these totally feminine cupcakes would be equally good made with raspberries, blackberries or a mix of fruits of the forest.

Preparation time: 30 minutes
(plus cooling and chilling)
Cooking time: 20 minutes
Makes: 12

Soured cream cupcakes

2 large eggs
150 ml (¼ pt) full fat soured cream
1 tsp vanilla essence
175 g (6 oz) unsalted butter, softened
175 g (6 oz) caster sugar
200 g (7 oz) self-raising flour

Strawberry frosting

50 g (2 oz) strawberries, hulled
100 g (4 oz) unsalted butter, softened
225 g (8 oz) icing sugar
12 extra strawberries and
sugar sprinkles, for decoration

1 To make the cupcakes, preheat the oven to 180°C/350F/gas mark 4. Line a 12-cup muffin tray with paper cases.

2 Whisk the eggs with 2 tablespoons of the soured cream and the vanilla essence.

3 Beat the butter and caster sugar together in a mixing bowl until creamy. Add the flour and remaining soured cream alternately with the egg mixture, beating or whisking until all the ingredients are evenly combined.

4 Transfer the mixture to a jug and pour into the paper cases. Bake for 20 minutes or until golden brown and a skewer pushed into the centre of a cake comes out clean. Cool in the tin for 10 minutes, before transferring to a wire rack to cool completely.

5 To make the frosting, mash the strawberries or push through a sieve to make a purée. Beat the butter in a bowl until creamy, then gradually sieve in the icing sugar, beating well after each addition. When all the icing sugar has been added, beat in the strawberry purée. Chill in the fridge to firm up.

6 Spread the frosting over the cupcakes. Make several cuts into each strawberry, fan the slices out and place on top of the cupcakes, adding a few sugar sprinkles for decoration.

 Tip

You can make your own soured cream by stirring 1 teaspoon lemon juice into 150 ml (¼ pt) double cream.

Hearts and flowers

Pretty as a picture, this modern version of a traditional wedding cake will make the happy couple's special day even more memorable. Use a mix of different sized cases so guests can choose which they prefer.

Preparation time: 30 minutes
(plus cooling and chilling)
Cooking time: 15–20 minutes
Makes 55–60 (using a mix of fairy cake, medium-size and standard muffin cases)

Honey and raspberry cupcakes

425 g (15 oz) unsalted butter, softened
225 g (8 oz) golden caster sugar
200 g (7 oz) clear honey
6 large eggs, beaten
675 g (1½ lb) self-raising flour
6 tbsp seedless raspberry jam
6 tbsp milk

White chocolate and vanilla frosting

275 g (10 oz) white chocolate, chopped
2 tbsp milk
140 g (5 oz) unsalted butter, softened
275 g (10 oz) icing sugar, sieved
1 tsp vanilla essence

To decorate

Small sugarpaste icing flowers
Pink and white sugared almonds
White and pink sparkle dust and sugar sprinkles

1 To make the cupcakes, preheat the oven to 180°C/350°F/gas mark 4. Line muffin and bun trays with around 55–60 paper cases of varying sizes.

2 In a large mixing bowl, beat together the butter and caster sugar until creamy. Beat in the honey until combined. Mix in the eggs, a little at a time, then fold in the flour. Finally stir in the jam and milk.

3 Spoon the mixture into the paper cases and bake for 15–20 minutes or until risen and springy to the touch. Cool in the trays for 10 minutes before removing the cupcakes to a wire rack to cool completely.

4 To make the frosting, melt the chocolate with the milk either on low heat in the microwave or by standing the bowl over a pan of steaming water, stirring occasionally until smooth. Beat the butter in another bowl until creamy and gradually beat in the icing sugar. Stir in the melted, cooled chocolate with the vanilla until you have a smooth icing. Chill in the refrigerator until firm enough to spread, stirring from time to time.

5 Spread the frosting over the cupcakes and decorate with small sugarpaste icing flowers, pink and white sugared almonds, white and pink sparkle dust and sugar sprinkles.

 Tip

The undecorated cakes can be frozen for up to 2 months before use. Bake and freeze in the trays until solid then pack into plastic bags or freezer boxes and seal tightly.

Sweet and lovely

For the bride looking for a bold, bright cake, these colourful cupcakes will delight her and her groom. As with Hearts and Flowers (see page 46), it's best to use a selection of different-sized paper cases.

Preparation time: 30 minutes
(plus cooling)
Cooking time: 15–20 minutes
Makes: 45–50 (using a mix of fairy cake, medium-size and standard muffin cases)

Double chocolate chip cupcakes

400 g (14 oz) unsalted butter, softened

400 g (14 oz) caster sugar

6 large eggs, beaten

400 g (14 oz) self-raising flour

200 g (7 oz) milk chocolate chunks

200 g (7 oz) dark chocolate chunks

Orange buttercream

175 g (6 oz) unsalted butter, softened

350 g (12 oz) icing sugar, sieved

2 tbsp orange juice

Pink, yellow and blue food colourings

To decorate

Small sweets, sugarpaste flowers, sugar sprinkles in various colours, top hats moulded from black sugarpaste, wedding rings moulded from white sugarpaste and painted with edible gold paint

1 To make the cupcakes, preheat the oven to 180°C/350°F/gas mark 4. Line muffin and bun trays with around 45–50 paper cases.

2 In a large mixing bowl, beat the butter and sugar together until creamy. Add the eggs a little at a time, beating well after each addition. Sieve in the flour and fold in until evenly mixed in. Finally stir in the milk and dark chocolate chunks.

3 Spoon the mixture into the paper cases and bake for 15–20 minutes or until risen and springy to the touch. Cool in the tins for 10 minutes before removing the cupcakes to a wire rack to cool completely.

4 To make the buttercream, beat the butter until creamy. Gradually sieve in the icing sugar, beating well after each addition, and stir in the orange juice until you have a smooth frosting. Spoon one third of the frosting into a separate bowl and another third into another bowl. Tint the three bowls of frosting pink, yellow and blue.

5 Spread the frostings over the cupcakes and decorate with small sweets, sugarpaste flowers, sugar sprinkles, top hats moulded from black sugarpaste and wedding rings moulded from white sugarpaste and painted with edible gold paint.

 Tip

Edible gold paint is available from cake decorating equipment shops and websites. Brush it over the sugarpaste wedding rings, adding several layers until the desired depth of colour has been achieved.

Cakes for kids

Baby shower

If you have time, you can mould the tiny toys and baby decorations yourself from marzipan or sugarpaste icing. If not shops and websites selling cake decorating equipment should offer a good choice of ready made ones. The rice flour gives the cupcakes a lighter, crumblier texture.

Preparation time: 25 minutes
(plus cooling)
Cooking time: 20–25 minutes
Makes: 12

Tangy lemon cupcakes
175 g (6 oz) unsalted butter, softened
175 g (6 oz) caster sugar
Finely grated rind of 2 unwaxed lemons
3 large eggs, beaten
175 g (6 oz) self-raising flour
50 g (2 oz) rice flour
Juice of 1 lemon

Lemon buttercream
115 g (4 oz) unsalted butter, softened
225 g (8 oz) icing sugar
About 2 tbsp lemon juice
Pink and blue food colourings (optional)

To decorate
Small edible toy or baby themed decorations
Sugar sprinkles

1 To make the cupcakes, preheat the oven to 180°C/350°F/gas mark 4. Line a 12-cup muffin tray with paper cases.

2 Beat the butter, sugar and lemon rind together until creamy. Add the eggs a little at a time, beating well after each addition. Fold in the self-raising and rice flours until evenly combined. Finally stir in the lemon juice.

3 Spoon the mixture into the cases and bake for 20–25 minutes or until golden brown and springy to the touch. Cool in the tin for 10 minutes before transferring to a wire rack to cool completely.

4 To make the buttercream, beat the butter until creamy. Gradually sieve in the icing sugar a little at a time, beating well after each addition and adding the lemon juice as needed so the icing is soft and smooth.

5 Tint the buttercream with a few drops of food colouring as desired and pipe or spread it over the cupcakes. Decorate with small edible toys or baby-themed decorations and sugar sprinkles.

 **Tip**

If you don't have any rice flour and don't want to buy a pack especially, increase the quantity of self-raising flour accordingly.

Sports mad

If your son – or daughter – is football mad you can decorate these little cakes with miniature footballs or a shirt in the colour of their favourite team. If soccer is not to their taste, the decorations can be replaced with ones for other sports such as a pair skis, a hockey stick, rugby ball, golf club, tennis racket or baseball bat and ball.

Preparation time: 25 minutes
(plus cooling)
Cooking time: 12–15 minutes
Makes: 20 (using fairy cake cases)

Chocolate and orange cupcakes

175 g (6 oz) unsalted butter, softened
175 g (6 oz) light muscovado sugar
Finely grated rind of 1 orange
3 large eggs, beaten
175 g (6 oz) self-raising flour
25 g (1 oz) cocoa powder
1 tbsp orange juice

Milk chocolate frosting

140 g (5 oz) milk chocolate chips
115 g (4 oz) unsalted butter, softened
225 g (8 oz) icing sugar
2 tbsp milk

To decorate

Edible sporting novelties, bought
or homemade
Sugar sprinkles

1 To make the cupcakes, preheat the oven to 180°C/350°F/gas mark 4. Line bun tins with fairy cake cases.

2 Beat the butter, muscovado sugar and orange rind together until creamy. Beat in the eggs, a little at a time, then sieve in the flour and cocoa powder and fold in until evenly combined. Stir in the orange juice.

3 Spoon the mixture into the paper cases and bake for 12–15 minutes or until risen and springy when pressed. Cool in the tins for 10 minutes, before removing to a wire rack to cool completely.

4 To make the frosting, put the chocolate chips in a bowl and melt by microwaving on full power for 1–2 minutes. Beat the butter until creamy and gradually sieve in the icing sugar, beating well after each addition. Once all the sugar has been added, beat in the melted chocolate and milk. Chill if necessary to firm up.

5 Spread the frosting over the cakes and decorate with edible novelties representing your child's favourite sport and sugar sprinkles.

Niobrara County Library
Luok, Wyoming 82225

 Tip

Shops or websites selling cake decorating equipment are almost certain to stock a range of sport-themed decorations, but you can have fun moulding your own from coloured almond paste or sugarpaste icing.

Animal magic

The faces of jungle favourites and family pets can be recreated from rolled out marzipan or sugarpaste icing. If you're not a proficient artist, use children's books, greeting cards and cartoons as inspiration and trace outlines on to greaseproof paper to use as a guide when cutting out the pieces.

Preparation time: 25 minutes
(plus cooling, chilling and decorating)
Cooking time: 20–25 minutes
Makes: 12

Fudge cupcakes

175 g (6 oz) unsalted butter, softened

175 g (6 oz) golden caster sugar

3 large eggs, beaten

175 g (6 oz) self-raising flour

50 g (2 oz) fudge, chopped into small pieces

Fudge icing

140 g (5 oz) fudge, chopped

50 g (2 oz) unsalted butter

3 tbsp milk

115 g (4 oz) icing sugar

To decorate

Animal faces such as cats, pigs, dogs, sheep, elephants and cows made from coloured marzipan or sugarpaste icing, and coloured decorating icing and white decorating icing for sheep

Chocolate sprinkles

1 To make the cupcakes, preheat the oven to 180°C/350°F/gas mark 4. Line a 12-cup muffin tray with paper cases.

2 Beat the butter and sugar together until creamy. Gradually beat in the eggs, then stir in the flour and fudge pieces until evenly combined.

3 Spoon into the paper cases and bake for 20–25 minutes or until golden brown and springy to the touch. Cool in the tray for 10 minutes before removing to a wire rack to cool completely.

4 To make the icing, put the fudge in a pan, add the butter and milk and heat gently, stirring constantly, until the fudge and butter melt. Remove the pan from the heat and sieve in the icing sugar. Stir briskly until the sugar is incorporated evenly into the melted ingredients. Leave to cool and thicken to a spreadable consistency.

5 Spread the icing over the cupcakes and decorate with animal faces and chocolate sprinkles.

 Tip

To make the animal faces, roll out coloured marzipan or sugarpaste icing and cut out the main shapes. Add details by cutting small pieces of marzipan or icing for ears, paws and feet, dampening and pressing into place. Add eyes and other details with coloured decorating icing. For sheep, make the face from marzipan or sugarpaste and press on top of the cupcakes. Add wool by piping white decorating icing around the face directly on the cakes.

Let's hear it for the girls

Little – and big – girls will love these girly cakes with their soft, sticky frosting. To ring the changes, one half of the cake mixture can be coloured green, blue, orange or any colour you like, or 1 tablespoon of cocoa powder can be stirred in to give a chocolate flavour.

Preparation time: 30 minutes
(plus cooling, chilling and decorating)
Cooking time: 15–20 minutes
Makes: 12

Marbled pink cupcakes

175 g (6 oz) unsalted butter, softened
175 g (6 oz) caster sugar
3 large eggs, beaten
1 tsp almond essence
175 g (6 oz) self-raising flour
Pink food colouring

Marshmallow frosting

140 g (5 oz) white or pink marshmallows
2 tbsp milk
2 egg whites
25 g (1 oz) caster sugar

To decorate

Sugar sprinkles
Small flowers made from coloured marzipan or sugar paste icing, bought or homemade
Butterflies piped with coloured writing icing

1 To make the cupcakes, preheat the oven to 180°C/350°F/gas mark 4. Line a 12-cup muffin tray with paper cases.

2 Beat the butter and sugar together until creamy. Gradually beat in the eggs, adding the almond essence with the last addition of egg. Stir in the flour until evenly combined.

3 Spoon half the mixture into another bowl and tint with a few drops of pink food colouring.

4 Spoon teaspoonfuls of the two mixtures alternately into the paper cases and bake for 15–20 minutes or until just firm to the touch. Cool in the tray for 10 minutes before removing the cupcakes to a wire rack to cool completely.

5 To make the marshmallow frosting, put the marshmallows and milk in a small pan and heat gently until melted. Stir until smooth and set aside to cool. In a mixing bowl, whisk the egg whites until standing in soft peaks, add the sugar and whisk again until stiff. Fold the melted marshmallows into the egg whites until evenly combined. Leave in the fridge to firm up, stirring from time to time.

6 Spread the frosting – which will be very sticky – over the cupcakes with a small palette knife or other round bladed knife and decorate with sugar sprinkles, small marzipan or sugarpaste flowers and butterflies piped with coloured writing icing. To make the butterflies, trace the outline of the butterfly wings on to baking parchment with a pencil and pipe over them with coloured writing icing. Pipe the body and head with black writing icing and add two white eyes. Push the ends of two flower stamens into the head for antennae. Leave to set hard before lifting off the parchment with a small palette knife.

Ugly bugs

Not really so ugly, especially if you pipe big, beaming smiles on the caterpillars' faces! You can of course make other creatures to top the cakes. Try beetles, frogs, spiders or coiled snakes – the more gruesome they are, the more the kids will love them!

Preparation time: 40 minutes
(plus cooling and decorating)
Cooking time: 10–12 minutes (mini cases) or 15–20 minutes (small cases)
Makes: 12 mini and 14 small cupcakes

Chocolate cupcakes

175 g (6 oz) unsalted butter, softened
175 g (6 oz) caster sugar
3 large eggs, beaten
140 g (5 oz) self-raising flour
50 g (2 oz) cocoa powder
1 tsp baking powder
1 tbsp milk

To decorate

4 tbsp apricot jam
350 g (12 oz) green-coloured marzipan or sugarpaste icing
Black and red writing icing
Small amounts of other coloured sugarpaste icings for making caterpillar antennae, ladybirds and bees

1 To make the cupcakes, preheat the oven to 180°C/350°F/gas mark 4. Line a 12-cup mini muffin tray with paper cases (or use a silicone tray) and bun trays with 14 small paper cases.

2 Beat the butter and sugar together until creamy. Gradually add the eggs, beating well after each addition. Sieve in the flour, cocoa powder and baking powder and stir in with the milk until evenly combined.

3 Spoon the mixture into the paper cases and bake the mini cakes for 10–12 minutes and the small ones for 15–20 minutes, or until just firm to the touch. Cool in the trays for 10 minutes before transferring to a wire rack to cool completely.

4 To decorate, heat the apricot jam until bubbling. Remove the mini cupcakes from their paper cases if necessary and brush all over with the hot jam. Roll out about two-thirds of the green marzipan or sugarpaste icing and use to cover the tops and sides of the cakes, pressing the icing over the jam to stick it in place and trimming the bottom edges neatly. Roll out the remaining green marzipan or icing, together with the trimmings. Brush the tops of the small cakes with warm jam, stamp out circles of marzipan or icing the same size as the tops of the cakes using a pastry cutter and lift over, pressing down gently.

5 Arrange the mini cakes in two wiggly lines of 6 cakes each for caterpillars and pipe on eyes, mouth and legs with coloured writing icing. Antennae can be made from small pieces of black sugarpaste icing and fixed in place with writing icing or short lengths of chocolate matchmaker sweets.

6 Model ladybirds and bumble bees from coloured marzipan or sugarpaste icing and fix on top of the small cakes with a dab of writing icing.

Chocolate and banana party cakes

Ask children what they most like to eat and the chances are chocolate and bananas will figure strongly amongst their favourites. These could be served as an alternative birthday cake with candles or lollypops decorating them.

Preparation time: 25 minutes
(plus cooling and chilling)
Cooking time: 12–15 minutes
Makes: 18 (using fairy cake cases)

Banana and chocolate cupcakes

115 g (4 oz) unsalted butter, softened
115 g (4 oz) light muscovado sugar
2 large eggs
1 small ripe banana, peeled and
roughly chopped (about 75g / 3oz
unpeeled weight)
1 tbsp milk
175 g (6 oz) self-raising flour
1 tbsp cocoa powder
50 g (2 oz) milk chocolate chips

White chocolate icing

140 g (5 oz) white chocolate chips
150 ml (¼ pt) double cream
Sugar sprinkles, chocolate sprinkles,
candles, jellybeans and lollypops
to decorate

1 To make the cupcakes, preheat the oven to 190ºC/375ºF/gas mark 5. Line bun trays with 18 paper cases.

2 Beat the butter and sugar together until creamy. Put the eggs, banana and milk in a liquidizer and blend until smooth. Stir into the butter and sugar mixture alternately with the flour and cocoa powder. Finally stir in the milk chocolate chips.

4 Spoon the mixture into the paper cases and bake for 12–15 minutes until firm to the touch. Leave to cool in the tin for 10 minutes before transferring to a wire rack to cool completely.

5 To make the icing, melt the white chocolate chips in a bowl over a pan of simmering water, stirring until smooth. Remove from the heat and stir in the double cream. Set aside in a cool place until the icing has thickened enough to spread.

6 Spread the icing over the cupcakes and decorate with sugar sprinkles, chocolate sprinkles, candles, jellybeans and lollypops.

 *Tip*

If you don't have a liquidizer, the banana can be mashed with a fork and beaten with the eggs and milk before being added to the cake mixture.

Fruits and flowers

Elderflower and raspberry

Elderflowers have the perfumed sweetness of ripe Muscat grapes and they are delicious in a syrup. The quantity of syrup made here is more than you'll need so store the excess in a sealed bottle or jar in the fridge and add it to frostings, sorbets, desserts and summer cocktails such as Pimm's.

Preparation time: 25 minutes (plus cooling)
Cooking time: 15–20 minutes
Makes 18 (using medium-size cases)

Elderflower syrup

Juice of 2 lemons
225 g (8 oz) golden caster sugar
4 heads of elderflowers

Raspberry cupcakes

175 g (6 oz) unsalted butter
175 g (6 oz) golden caster sugar
Finely grated zest of 1 lemon
3 large eggs, beaten
40 g (1½ oz) ground hazelnuts
140 g (5 oz) fresh raspberries
175 g (6 oz) self-raising flour
1 tsp baking powder
2 tbsp milk
200 ml (7 fl oz) double cream
Extra raspberries and mint or lemon balm leaves, for decoration

1 To make the syrup, put the lemon juice in a saucepan, add 250 ml (8 fl oz) cold water and stir in the sugar. Heat gently until the sugar dissolves, then bring to the boil and simmer for 1 minute.

2 Rinse the elderflowers thoroughly to remove any insects and snip the heads into smaller sprigs with kitchen scissors. Add to the syrup, stir well, remove from the heat and cover the pan. Set aside for several hours so the syrup has time to absorb the flavour and scent of the elderflowers.

3 Preheat the oven to 180°C/350°F/gas mark 4. Line muffin trays with 18 medium-size paper cases.

4 To make the cupcakes, beat the butter and sugar together in a mixing bowl until creamy. Beat in the lemon zest and then gradually beat in the eggs. Stir in the ground hazelnuts.

5 Gently crush the raspberries and dust with a little of the flour. Stir the remaining flour, baking powder and milk into the creamed mixture and fold in the raspberries until everything is evenly combined.

6 Spoon into the paper cases and bake for 15–20 minutes or until golden brown and just firm to the touch. Allow the cupcakes to cool in the tin for 10 minutes before lifting them out on to a wire rack to cool completely.

7 Whip the cream until it starts to thicken. Drain the elderflower syrup and add 2 tablespoons of it to the cream. Whisk again until the cream holds its shape. Pipe or spread over the tops of the cupcakes and decorate with the extra raspberries and small mint or lemon balm leaves.

Pistachio, rosewater and grenadine

Rosewater is widely used in Middle Eastern cooking as the large, fragrant damask roses that are used to make it grow there in abundance. It is added to Turkish delight and marzipan as well as the Indian yoghurt drink lassi, and makes a delicate, summery flavouring for cakes.

Preparation time: 20 minutes
(plus cooling)
Cooking time: 15–20 minutes
Makes: 12

Cupcakes

175 g (6 oz) unsalted butter, softened
175 g (6 oz) caster sugar
3 large eggs, beaten
175 g (6 oz) self-raising flour
1 tbsp rosewater
50 g (2 oz) shelled pistachios,
finely ground
1 tbsp milk

Grenadine buttercream

75 g (3 oz) unsalted butter, softened
175 g (6 oz) icing sugar
1–2 tbsp grenadine

To decorate

2 tbsp finely chopped pistachios
Frosted rose petals

1 To make the cupcakes, preheat the oven to 180°C/350°F/gas mark 4. Line a 12-cup muffin tray with paper cases.

2 Beat the butter and sugar together in a mixing bowl until creamy. Gradually beat in the eggs a little at a time and then stir in the flour, followed by the rosewater, pistachios and milk.

3 Spoon the mixture into the cases and bake for 15–20 minutes until golden and a skewer comes out clean when pushed into the centre of a cake. Cool in the tin for 10 minutes, then remove to a wire rack to cool completely.

4 To make the buttercream, beat the butter until smooth. Gradually sieve in the icing sugar, beating after each addition. Stir in enough grenadine to produce a soft pink frosting that can be piped or spread over the cakes.

5 Cover the tops of the cupcakes with the buttercream, sprinkle with the chopped pistachios and decorate with frosted rose petals.

 Tip

Frosted rose petals can be bought from larger supermarkets or you can make your own. Brush rose petals (from flowers that have been organically grown with no insecticide sprayed on them) lightly with egg white and dust with caster sugar. Place on a plate lined with kitchen paper and leave to dry.

Blackcurrant and borage

Borage, or starflower as it is sometimes called, with its vivid blue, pointed flowers might be one of the prettiest herbs but it is not always the gardener's favourite as once established it spreads rapidly taking over the flowerbed. Traditional folklore says that borage helps dispel depression and lift the spirits so if you're feeling down, these cupcakes could be just what you need.

Preparation time: 20 minutes (plus cooling)
Cooking time: 15–20 minutes
Makes: 18 (using medium-size cases)

Cupcakes

140 g (5 oz) blackcurrants
175 g (6 oz) self-raising flour
175 g (6 oz) unsalted butter, softened
175 g (6 oz) caster sugar
3 large eggs, beaten
1 tsp baking powder
2 tbsp orange juice
1 tsp finely chopped young, fresh borage leaves

Icing

175 g (6 oz) icing sugar
2–3 tbsp blackcurrant juice or blackcurrant juice drink
Frosted borage flowers and extra blackcurrants

1 To make the cupcakes, pull the blackcurrants off their stalks using a fork and crush them lightly. Dust with a little of the flour. Preheat the oven to 180°C/350°F/gas mark 4. Line muffin trays with 18 medium-size paper cases.

2 Beat the butter and sugar together in a mixing bowl until creamy. Gradually beat in the eggs and then stir in the rest of the flour, the baking powder, orange juice and borage leaves until evenly combined. Finally stir in the blackcurrants.

3 Spoon the mixture into the paper cases and bake for 15–20 minutes or until golden brown and springy when pressed. Leave in the tins for 10 minutes to cool, then lift out and place on a wire rack.

4 When the cupcakes are cold, sieve the icing sugar into a bowl and stir in enough blackcurrant juice or juice drink to give a smooth, spreadable consistency. Spread the icing over the cupcakes and decorate each one with frosted borage flowers and extra blackcurrants.

 *Tip*

To frost borage flowers, brush the tops of the flowers with lightly beaten egg white and dust with caster sugar. Leave on a plate lined with kitchen paper to dry.

Orange, buttermilk and sunflower

Shops selling cake decorating equipment and larger supermarkets will stock a range of small flowers made from royal icing or sugarpaste that can be used to decorate cupcakes. You can also make your own such as the sunflowers shown here using flower cutters and piped chocolate.

Preparation time: 30 minutes (plus cooling)
Cooking time: 20–25 minutes
Makes: 12

Cupcakes

115 g (4 oz) unsalted butter, softened
175 g (6 oz) caster sugar
Grated zest of 1 small orange
225 g (8 oz) plain flour
1 tsp baking powder
1 tsp bicarbonate of soda
3 large eggs, beaten
225 ml (8 fl oz) buttermilk
2 tbsp sunflower seeds

Frosting

65g (2½ oz) unsalted butter, softened
140 g (5 oz) icing sugar
1 tbsp orange juice
Orange food colouring (optional)
Bought or homemade icing or marzipan flowers, to decorate

1 To make the cupcakes, preheat the oven to 180°C/350°F/gas mark 4. Line a 12-cup muffin tray with paper cases.

2 Beat the butter, sugar and orange zest together in a mixing bowl until creamy. Sieve together the flour, baking powder and bicarbonate of soda.

3 Gradually beat in the eggs and then stir in the flour, buttermilk and sunflower seeds until evenly combined.

4 Spoon into the paper cases and bake for 20–25 minutes until golden and a skewer pushed into the centre of a cake comes out clean. Cool in the tin for 10 minutes before removing to a wire rack to cool completely.

5 To make the frosting, beat the butter until smooth. Sieve in the icing sugar a little at a time, beating well after each addition. Stir in enough orange juice to give a soft icing and tint with a few drops of orange food colouring.

6 Spread or pipe the icing over the cupcakes and decorate with bought or homemade icing or marzipan flowers.

 *Tip*

If you're making the frosting during warm weather and it is a little soft, chill in the fridge for 30 minutes or until it becomes firm enough to spread.

Lavender and lemon

These delicately flavoured cupcakes make the perfect accompaniment to a pot of Earl Grey tea on a summer's day. If serving as part of a teatime selection of cakes, use 12 fairy cake paper cases and reduce the baking time by about 5 minutes.

Preparation time: 20 minutes
(plus cooling)
Cooking time: 20 minutes
Makes: 8

Cupcakes

75 ml (3 fl oz) milk
6 lavender flower heads, plus extra sprigs for decoration
140 g (5 oz) unsalted butter
140 g (5 oz) caster sugar
Grated rind of 1 small lemon
2 large eggs, beaten
140 g (5 oz) self-raising flour
115 g (4 oz) icing sugar
Few drops of violet or mauve food colouring

1 Put the milk in a small pan, add the lavender flower heads and bring gently to a simmer or heat in a bowl in the microwave. Remove from the heat, cover and set aside for 30 minutes, then strain and discard the lavender.

2 Preheat the oven to 180°C/350°F/gas mark 4. Line a muffin tray with paper cases.

3 Beat the butter, caster sugar and lemon rind together until soft and creamy. Beat in the eggs a little at a time and then stir in the flour. Stir in 2 tablespoons of the lavender milk to soften the mixture.

4 Spoon into the paper cases and bake for 20 minutes or until golden brown and springy to the touch. Cool in the tin for 10 minutes, before lifting out carefully and placing on a wire rack to cool completely.

5 Sieve the icing sugar into a bowl and stir in enough of the remaining lavender milk to make a smooth icing. Tint with 1 or 2 drops of violet or mauve food colouring.

6 Spoon or spread the icing over the cupcakes and decorate with small sprigs of lavender flowers.

 ## Tip

It is important to use lavender flowers that have either been grown organically without being sprayed by pesticides or lavender specifically designed for culinary use. The latter can be bought from specialist cook shops or over the internet.

A taste of the exotic

Mango and palm sugar

Palm sugar, also known as jaggery, is a raw sugar popular in Asian cooking that is usually made from cane sugar and coconut palm sap. The sap is boiled down until it crystallizes and the resulting sugar is either sold as large granules or a solid ball that crumbles easily. If you use the granular sugar, it won't dissolve when creamed with the butter but will break down during baking.

Preparation time: 25 minutes (plus cooling and decorating)
Cooking time: 20–25 minutes
Makes: 12

Mango cupcakes

175 g (6 oz) unsalted butter, softened
115 g (4 oz) caster sugar
50 g (2 oz) palm sugar
3 large eggs, beaten
175 g (6 oz) self-raising flour
50 g (2 oz) dried mango, chopped
1 tbsp milk or fruit juice (such as orange or mango)

Frosting

75 g (3 oz) unsalted butter, softened
175 g (6 oz) icing sugar
1–2 tbsp milk
Yellow and blue food colourings

To decorate

Palm trees cut from green and brown sugarpaste icing, suns cut from yellow sugarpaste and yellow writing icing, sun umbrellas cut from coloured sugarpaste and black writing icing, palm sugar

1 To make the cupcakes, preheat the oven to 180°C/350°F/gas mark 4. Line a 12-cup muffin tray with paper cases.

2 Beat the butter, caster sugar and palm sugar together until creamy and evenly combined. Beat in the eggs a little at a time and then stir in the flour. Finally stir in the dried mango and milk or juice.

3 Spoon the mixture into the paper cases and bake for 20–25 minutes or until a skewer comes out clean when pushed into the centre of a cake. Cool in the tray for 10 minutes before removing to a wire rack to cool completely.

4 To make the frosting, beat the butter until smooth, then gradually sieve in the icing sugar, beating well after each addition. Stir in the milk. Transfer half the frosting to another bowl and colour one half yellow and the other blue. Spread the icing over the cupcakes.

5 Decorate with palm trees cut from green and brown sugarpaste, tropical suns cut from yellow sugarpaste with rays piped using yellow writing icing, sun umbrellas cut from coloured sugarpaste with the poles piped using black writing icing and sandy beaches of palm sugar.

 Tip

If you're unable to find palm sugar, substitute demerara or light muscovado sugar instead.

Piña colada

Not quite a cocktail in a paper case but a special treat none the less. If you prefer not to use alcohol in the frosting, pineapple juice or coconut cream will both work equally well.

Preparation time: 25 minutes
Cooking time: 20–25 minutes
Makes: 12

Pineapple and coconut cupcakes

175 g (6 oz) unsalted butter, softened
175 g (6 oz) golden caster sugar
3 large eggs, beaten
75 g (3 oz) fresh pineapple or 2 rings canned in juice, chopped into small pieces
175 g (6 oz) self-raising flour
50 g (2 oz) desiccated coconut
2 tbsp coconut cream, light rum or Malibu

Rum frosting

115 g (4 oz) unsalted butter, softened
225 g (8 oz) icing sugar
2 tbsp light rum or Malibu
Blue and yellow sugar sprinkles, to decorate

1 To make the cupcakes, preheat the oven to 180°C/350°F/gas mark 4. Line a 12-cup muffin tray with paper cases.

2 Beat the butter and sugar together until creamy. Gradually mix in the eggs, beating well after each addition. Dust the pineapple pieces in a little of the flour and stir into the creamed mixture with the rest of the flour, the desiccated coconut and the coconut cream, light rum or Malibu

3 Spoon into the paper cases and bake for 20–25 minutes or until a skewer pushed into the centre of one of the cakes comes out clean. Cool in the tray for 10 minutes before removing to a wire rack to cool completely.

4 To make the frosting, beat the butter until creamy. Gradually sieve in the icing sugar, beating well after each addition. Stir in the rum or Malibu, pipe or spread the frosting over the cupcakes and decorate with blue and yellow sugar sprinkles.

Niobrara County Library
Lusk, Wyoming 82225

 Tip

Creamed coconut is thicker than ordinary coconut milk and is available as a liquid in cartons or in block form. If you use the latter, grate about 40 g (1½ oz) of the coconut block into a bowl and add a little boiling water to dissolve it to a thick cream.

Strawberry daiquiri

The first daiquiri cocktail was mixed around 1900 when Jennings Cox, an American mining engineer who was working in Cuba, added fresh lime juice and sugar to the local rum as his supply of gin had run dry. Since then numerous variations on the classic mix have been shaken by bartenders around the globe, but whether any have attempted a cupcake daiquiri is not recorded.

Preparation time: 25 minutes
(plus cooling)
Cooking time: 20–25 minutes
Makes: 15

Cupcakes

175 g (6 oz) unsalted butter, softened
175 g (6 oz) light muscovado sugar
Finely grated rind of 2 limes
3 large eggs, beaten
225 g (8 oz) strawberries, hulled
and chopped
140 g (5 oz) plain flour
140 g (5 oz) self-raising flour
2 tbsp lime juice

Lime and rum frosting

115 g (4 oz) unsalted butter, softened
225 g (8 oz) icing sugar
Finely grated rind of 1 lime
2 tbsp light rum or lime juice
Extra strawberries, sliced, and
sugar sprinkles, to decorate

1 To make the cupcakes, preheat the oven to 180°C/350°F/gas mark 4. Line muffin trays with 15 paper cases.

2 Beat the butter, sugar and lime zest together until creamy. Gradually mix in the eggs, beating well after each addition. Dust the strawberries with a little of the plain flour and stir into the creamed mixture with the rest of the plain flour, the self-raising flour and the lime juice.

3 Spoon into the paper cases and bake for 20–25 minutes or until a skewer pushed into the centre of one of the cakes comes out clean. Cool in the tray for 10 minutes before removing to a wire rack to cool completely.

4 To make the frosting, beat the butter until creamy. Sieve in the icing sugar, a little at a time, beating well after each addition. Stir in the lime zest and rum or lime juice.

5 Spread the frosting over the cupcakes and decorate with strawberry slices and sugar sprinkles.

 *Tip*

Top the cupcakes with the strawberry slices just before serving or they may leak juice that will melt the sugar sprinkles.

Pineapple and lime

Fresh or tinned pineapple can be used to make these cupcakes but if using tinned, opt for fruit in juice rather than syrup and drain it well on kitchen paper before chopping into small pieces.

Preparation time: 30 minutes
(plus cooling)
Cooking time: 20 minutes
Makes: 12

Cupcakes

140 g (5 oz) light muscovado sugar
2 large eggs
Finely grated rind of 1 lime
115 ml (4 fl oz) sunflower oil
140 g (5 oz) pineapple, peeled weight,
fresh or tinned, chopped into small pieces
175 g (6 oz) self-raising flour

Frosting

40 g (1½ oz) unsalted butter, softened
140 g (5 oz) full fat cream cheese
2 tsp lime juice
2 tbsp pineapple jam
Crystallised pineapple, to decorate

1 To make the cupcakes, preheat the oven to 180°C/350°F/gas mark 4. Line a 12-cup muffin tray with paper cases.

2 In a mixing bowl, whisk the muscovado sugar, eggs and lime rind together until evenly combined using an electric whisk. Add the oil in a thin stream, whisking all the time so it is incorporated evenly into the egg mixture. Dust the pineapple pieces in a little of the flour.

3 Stir in the rest of the flour and the pineapple. Spoon the mixture into the paper cases and bake for about 20 minutes or until a skewer pushed into the centre of one of the cakes comes out clean.

4 Cool in the tin for 10 minutes before transferring to a wire rack to cool completely.

5 To make the frosting, whisk together the butter, cream cheese and lime juice until smooth. Stir in the pineapple jam.

6 Spread the frosting over the cupcakes and decorate with crystallised pineapple.

 Tip

You can buy crystallised pineapple but it's very easy to make your own. Dissolve 115 g (4 oz) caster sugar in 115 ml (4 fl oz) water, bring to the boil and add 3 thin pineapple rings or slices. Lower the heat and simmer until the pineapple is transparent and starting to caramelize. Drain well, snip into small pieces and dust with caster sugar. Any leftover can be stored in an airtight container.

Coconut and passion fruit

Coconut makes these cupcakes deliciously moist and the fragrant passion fruit icing adds to their exotic flavour. It's not worth buying a tin of coconut milk especially, but if you have an opened one in the fridge that needs using up substitute this for the ordinary milk.

Preparation time: 30 minutes
(plus cooling)
Cooking time: 20 minutes
Makes: 15 (using medium-size cases)

Cupcakes

115 g (4 oz) unsalted butter, softened
140 g (5 oz) golden caster sugar
2 large eggs
140 g (5 oz) self-raising flour
100 g (3½ oz) desiccated coconut
2 tbsp milk or coconut milk

Icing

3 passion fruit
140 g (5 oz) icing sugar
Toasted coconut shavings, to decorate

1 To make the cupcakes, preheat the oven to 180°C/350°F/gas mark 4. Line muffin trays with 15 medium-size paper cases.

2 Put the butter, golden caster sugar, eggs, flour, desiccated coconut and milk or coconut milk into a bowl and beat with a hand whisk or wooden spoon until the mixture is smooth and creamy. Alternatively, put the ingredients in a food processor and blend until smooth.

3 Spoon the mixture into the paper cases and bake for about 20 minutes or until golden brown and springy to the touch.

4 Cool in the tin for 10 minutes before transferring to a wire rack to cool completely.

5 To make the icing, halve the passion fruits, scoop out the pulp and seeds of one and add to the icing sugar. Scoop out the pulp and seeds from the other two into a small bowl. Heat gently until the seeds separate from the pulp, then push through a sieve and stir the pulp into the icing sugar until evenly mixed in.

6 Spoon the icing over the cupcakes and top with a few toasted coconut shavings.

 Tip

If preferred, the pulp and seeds of all three passion fruit can be stirred directly into the icing sugar or the seeds of all three sieved out. Heating the pulp and seeds makes it easier to separate them.

Spoil yourself

Tiramisu and mascarpone

Italy's favourite dessert transformed into melt-in-the-mouth cupcakes that will be an instant hit at any coffee or tea party. The coffee liqueur Tia Maria adds a kick to the frosting but substitute strong black coffee if you prefer.

Preparation time: 25 minutes
(plus cooling)
Cooking time: 15–20 minutes
Makes: 12

Tiramisu cupcakes

175 g (6 oz) unsalted butter, softened
175 g (6 oz) dark muscovado sugar
3 large eggs, beaten
175 g (6 oz) self-raising flour
2 tbsp strong black coffee

Mascarpone frosting

115 g (4 oz) mascarpone
325 g (11 oz) icing sugar
75 g (3 oz) unsalted butter, softened
1 tbsp Tia Maria or strong black coffee

To decorate

50 g (2 oz) dark chocolate, melted
Chocolate coffee beans
Vermicelli

1 To make the cupcakes, preheat the oven to 180ºC/350ºF/gas mark 4. Line a 12-cup muffin tray with paper cases.

2 Beat the butter and sugar together until creamy and then beat in the eggs a little at a time, beating well between each addition. Stir in the flour and coffee until evenly combined.

3 Spoon the mixture into the paper cases and bake for 15–20 minutes or until a skewer pushed into the centre of one of the cakes comes out clean. Cool in the tray for 10 minutes before removing to a wire rack to cool completely.

4 To make the frosting, whisk together the mascarpone, icing sugar, butter and Tia Maria or coffee until smooth and creamy. Pipe or spread over the cupcakes.

5 To decorate, spoon the melted chocolate into a small paper piping bag, snip off the end and pipe the chocolate over the top of the cupcakes. Top each one with a chocolate coffee bean and sprinkle with vermicelli.

 *Tip*

If you don't have an espresso machine, strong black coffee can be made by stirring 2 tablespoons of hot water into 1 tablespoon of instant coffee powder or granules until the coffee dissolves.

Banoffee and toffee fudge

Dulce de leche, meaning 'sweet milk', is practically Argentina's national dish, being made from the milk produced by the famous pampas cattle. Available in jars in larger supermarkets, it is a smooth, creamy caramel spread that is irresistible spooned over ice cream, fresh fruit or added to frostings for cakes.

Preparation time: 30 minutes
(plus cooling)
Cooking time: 20 minutes
Makes: 12

Banoffee cupcakes

175 g (6 oz) unsalted butter, softened

75 g (3 oz) golden caster sugar

5 tbsp dulce de leche

3 large eggs

1 large or 2 small bananas (about 175 g / 6 oz unpeeled weight), peeled and chopped

200 g (7 oz) self-raising flour

1 tsp baking powder

Toffee fudge frosting

175 g (6 oz) unsalted butter, softened

350 g (12 oz) icing sugar

3 tbsp dulce de leche

To decorate

Chocolate sprinkles

Small pieces of fudge or soft toffee

Caramel shapes

1 To make the cupcakes, preheat the oven to 180°C/350°F/gas mark 4. Line a 12-cup muffin tray with paper cases.

2 Beat the butter and sugar together until creamy and stir in the dulce de leche. Liquidize the eggs and bananas together until smooth and stir into the creamed mixture alternately with the flour and baking powder.

3 Spoon into the paper cases and bake for 20 minutes or until a skewer pushed into the centre of one of the cakes comes out clean. Cool in the tray for 10 minutes before removing to a wire rack to cool completely.

4 To make the frosting, beat the butter until creamy. Gradually sieve in the icing sugar, beating well after each addition, and stir in the dulce de leche. Spoon or pipe the frosting over the cupcakes.

5 Decorate each one with chocolate sprinkles, small pieces of fudge or soft toffee and caramel shapes.

 Tip

To make the caramel shapes, line a board or baking sheet with baking parchment. Melt 115 g (4 oz) granulated sugar with 2 tablespoons water in a pan over a gentle heat, stirring until the sugar dissolves. Bring to the boil and keep boiling hard until the syrup turns a golden amber colour. Drizzle shapes of caramel on to the parchment with a spoon and leave to set hard. Lift off carefully with a palette knife and use to decorate the cupcakes.

Chocca-mocca and peppermint

Chocolate and peppermint are natural partners and these cupcakes with their soft, pastel green icing have the added kick of black coffee. Top them with your favourite chocolate peppermint sweets for extra indulgence.

Preparation time: 20 minutes (plus cooling)

Cooking time: 15 minutes

Makes: 12

Chocca-mocca cupcakes

225 g (8 oz) self-raising flour

½ tsp bicarbonate of soda

2 large eggs

175 g (6 oz) dark muscovado sugar

115 g (4 oz) unsalted butter, cubed and softened

2 tbsp cocoa powder and 2 tbsp instant coffee granules, dissolved in 225 ml (8 fl oz) boiling water and cooled

Peppermint frosting

75 g (3 oz) unsalted butter, softened

175 g (6 oz) icing sugar

1–2 tbsp milk

Few drops of peppermint essence and green food colouring

Chocolate peppermint creams, to decorate

1 To make the cupcakes, preheat the oven to 180°C/350°F/gas mark 4. Line a 12-cup muffin tray with paper cases.

2 Sieve together the flour and bicarbonate of soda. Put the eggs and muscovado sugar in a food processor or liquidiser and blend until smooth. Add the butter, blend again and then add the dissolved cocoa and coffee with half the flour mixture. Blend, add the rest of the flour mix and blend again until smooth. Transfer the mixture to a jug.

3 Pour the mixture into the paper cases to fill by two-thirds and bake for 15 minutes or until well risen and a skewer comes out clean when pushed into the centre of a cake. Cool in the tray for 10 minutes before removing to a wire rack to cool completely.

4 For the frosting, beat the butter until creamy and then gradually sieve in the icing sugar, beating well between each addition. Soften to a spreadable consistency by beating in a little milk. Flavour with a few drops of peppermint essence and tint pale green with food colouring.

5 Spread the frosting over the cupcakes and decorate with chocolate peppermint creams.

 Tip

If you don't have a food processor, beat the butter and sugar together until creamy. Gradually beat in the eggs and then stir in the flour mixture alternately with the dissolved cocoa and coffee.

Citrus drizzle and crunchy macadamia

Native to Australia, macadamia nuts have such a rich, buttery flavour it's not difficult to see why they are often compared to shortbread. Virtually always sold ready-shelled, their outer casing is so hard a special cracker is needed to break through it.

Preparation time: 20 minutes
(plus cooling)
Cooking time: 15–20 minutes
Makes: 12

Citrus drizzle cupcakes

200 g (7 oz) plain flour
2 tsp baking powder
125 g (4½ oz) unsalted butter, cubed and softened
200 g (7 oz) golden caster sugar
Grated rind of 1 lemon and 2 limes
2 large eggs
300 ml (½ pt) buttermilk

Macadamia crust

50 g (2 oz) plain flour
25 g (1 oz) unsalted butter
5 tbsp golden caster sugar
50 g (2 oz) macadamia nuts, chopped
Juice of 1 lemon and 2 limes

1 To make the cupcakes, preheat the oven to 180°C/350°F/gas mark 4. Line a 12-cup muffin tray with paper cases.

2 Sieve the flour and baking powder into a mixing bowl. Add the butter and rub into the dry ingredients until the mixture resembles coarse crumbs. Stir in the sugar.

3 In a large jug, beat together the lemon rind, lime rind, eggs and buttermilk. Pour into the bowl and beat or whisk everything together until evenly combined. Return the mixture to the jug and pour into the paper cases.

4 To make the crust, rub the flour and butter together until the mixture resembles coarse crumbs. Stir in 1 tablespoon of the sugar and the macadamias. Sprinkle the topping over the mixture in the cases.

5 Bake for 15–20 minutes or until a skewer pushed into the centre of a cake comes out clean. Mix the remaining sugar with the lemon and lime juice and spoon over the cupcakes as soon as they come out of the oven.

6 Leave to cool in the tin for 10 minutes before removing to a wire rack. Eat while still warm or leave to cool completely.

 Tip

Instead of macadamias, the topping can be made with almonds, cashews, hazelnuts or Brazil nuts.

Peach melba

In the early 1890s, the legendary French chef Escoffier created his peach melba dessert for the Australian soprano Dame Nellie Melba when head chef at the Savoy Hotel in London. Still as popular today – there is even a National Peach Melba Day celebrated each year on January 13 in the United States – the classic combination of peaches and raspberries makes a gorgeous cupcake with the ice cream being replaced by whipped cream.

Preparation time: 25 minutes (plus cooling)
Cooking time: 20 minutes
Makes: 12

Peach cupcakes

175 g (6 oz) unsalted butter, softened
140 g (5 oz) caster sugar
3 large eggs, beaten
175 g (6 oz) self-raising flour
1 tbsp milk
3 tbsp peach jam

To decorate

200 ml (7 fl oz) double or whipping cream
1 tsp vanilla essence
1 fresh peach and a few raspberries
Sugar sprinkles

1 To make the cupcakes, preheat the oven to 180°C/350°F/gas mark 4. Line a 12-cup muffin tray with paper cases.

2 Beat the butter until smooth, then beat in the caster sugar until light and creamy. Gradually beat in the eggs and then stir in the flour, milk and jam.

3 Spoon the mixture into the paper cases and bake for about 20 minutes or until risen and springy to the touch. Cool in the tray for 10 minutes before removing to a wire rack to cool completely.

4 To decorate, whip the cream with the vanilla until just holding its shape and spread over the cupcakes. Top with peach slices, raspberries and a scattering of sugar sprinkles.

 *Tip*

As the cupcakes are topped with fresh cream they need to be stored in the fridge until ready to serve.

Fruits of the forest

These cupcakes can be made using fresh or defrosted frozen berry fruits and you can make them with any combination you wish. Blackberries, raspberries, strawberries, blueberries and currants all work well and the richly flavoured little cupcakes are delicious served warm with a cup of tea.

Preparation time: 20 minutes (plus cooling)
Cooking time: 20 minutes
Makes: 12

Fruit cupcakes

75 g (3 oz) plain flour
200 g (7 oz) icing sugar
140 g (5 oz) ground almonds
Grated zest of 1 lemon
5 egg whites
175 g (6 oz) unsalted butter, melted and cooled
175 g (6 oz) mixed fruits of the forest, hulls and stalks removed as necessary

1 Preheat the oven to 200°C/400°F/gas mark 6. Line a 12-cup muffin tray with paper cases.

2 Sieve the flour and icing sugar into a bowl and stir in the ground almonds and lemon zest. Whisk the egg whites until standing in soft peaks, stir 1 tablespoon into the dry ingredients and then fold in the rest. Drizzle about one-third of the melted butter over the mixture and fold in, before adding the second and final third in the same way.

3 Spoon the mixture into the paper cases and top with the fruits.

4 Bake for 20 minutes or until a skewer pushed into the centre of one of the cakes comes out clean. Cool in the tin for 10 minutes before removing to a wire rack. Eat warm or cold.

 *Tip*

Halve or quarter any larger fruits such as blackberries or strawberries before scattering over the cakes.

Apricot, almond and amaretti

Amaretto Disarrono is a bitter-sweet liqueur from Lombardy in Italy made from herbs and fruits that have been steeped in apricot kernel oil. A popular addition to cocktails, it is sold in a distinctive rectangular bottle crafted by the master glassblowers of the island of Murano in the Venetian lagoon.

Preparation time: 30 minutes (plus cooling)
Cooking time: 20–25 minutes
Makes: 16

Apricot and almond cupcakes

140 g (5 oz) unsalted butter, softened
140 g (5 oz) caster sugar
2 large eggs, beaten
250 g (9 oz) self-raising flour
75 g (3 oz) ground almonds
125 ml (4½ fl oz) milk
1 tsp almond essence
3 tbsp apricot jam

Amaretti frosting

5 tbsp apricot jam
125 g (4½ oz) unsalted butter, softened
250 g (9 oz) icing sugar
2 tbsp Amaretto Disaronno liqueur (or ½ tsp almond essence and 2 tbsp milk)
Small amaretti or ratafia biscuits and sugar sprinkles, to decorate

1 To make the cupcakes, preheat the oven to 180°C/350°F/gas mark 4. Line muffin trays with 16 paper cases.

2 Beat the butter and sugar together until creamy. Gradually beat in the eggs, beating well after each addition, and then mix in the flour and ground almonds. Stir in the milk and almond essence. Add the apricot jam and stir until the mixture is streaked with the jam but not quite mixed in.

3 Spoon into the paper cases and bake for 20–25 minutes or until a skewer pushed into the centre of one of the cakes comes out clean. Cool in the tray for 10 minutes before removing the cupcakes to a wire rack to cool completely.

4 Using a small sharp knife, cut a small piece out of the top of each cake and spoon in a little apricot jam. Trim the base of the cut out pieces and gently press back in place.

5 To make the frosting, beat the butter until creamy. Gradually sieve in the icing sugar, beating well after each addition. Stir in the Amaretto liqueur or almond essence and milk.

6 Spread the frosting over the cupcakes and top each with a small amaretti or ratafia biscuit and sugar sprinkles.

Tip

Buy economy apricot jam to make the cupcakes as it will have fewer chunks of fruit than more expensive preserves. Remove any large pieces of fruit from the jam before spooning it into the holes cut into the cakes.

Size matters

Chocolate and cherry mini bites

Gold leaf will turn these tiny chocolate cupcakes into an A-list gourmet treat, adding that all important 'wow' factor to the finale of a special dinner. Available from specialist food suppliers, gold leaf is expensive to buy but only a very little is needed to decorate each cake.

Preparation time: 20 minutes (plus standing, cooling and setting)
Cooking time: 10–12 minutes
Makes: 30 (using mini cases)

Mini bites

50 g (2 oz) dried sour cherries
2 tbsp kirsch or brandy
50 g (2 oz) self-raising flour
25 g (1 oz) cocoa powder
75 g (3 oz) unsalted butter, cubed and softened
75 g (3 oz) dark muscovado sugar
3 large eggs, beaten

Icing

75 g (3 oz) crème fraîche
175 g (6 oz) dark chocolate, chopped
30 fresh cherries and 1 small sheet of edible gold leaf, to decorate

1 To make the mini bites, put the dried cherries in a small bowl and add the kirsch or brandy. Set aside for 30 minutes.

2 Preheat the oven to 180°C/350°F/gas mark 4. Line mini-muffin trays with 30 paper cases.

3 Sieve the flour and cocoa into a bowl. Add the butter, sugar and eggs and beat or whisk until you have a smooth mixture. Stir in the cherries and their soaking liquid.

4 Spoon the mixture into the paper cases, making sure you get a dried cherry in each cake, and bake for 10–12 minutes or until just firm to the touch. Leave in the trays for 10 minutes before removing to a wire rack to cool completely.

5 To make the icing, heat the crème fraîche and chocolate together in a pan over a very gentle heat, stirring until smooth. Chill in the fridge until the icing becomes thick enough to spread or pipe, stirring occasionally.

6 Spoon the icing over the cupcakes or pipe of blob on each one. Top with fresh cherries with their stalks still on. Pull off tiny pieces of edible gold leaf using tweezers and place on the cherries.

 *Tip*

The cakes can be baked ahead and frozen (undecorated) for up to 2 months.

Cappuccino with espresso frosting

A box of these tiny cupcakes decorated with chocolate coffee beans and crunchy demerara sugar would make a delightful gift for a dinner party host instead of the more usual bottle of wine. To make them even more special, the cupcakes could be topped with silver covered almonds or chocolate dragées, available from specialist food stores.

Preparation time: 25 minutes (plus cooling)
Cooking time: 12–15 minutes
Makes: 36 (using mini cases)

Mini cupcakes

115 g (4 oz) dark chocolate, chopped
2 tsp instant coffee granules or powder
115 g (4 oz) unsalted butter, softened
115 g (4 oz) dark muscovado sugar
2 large eggs, beaten
175 g (6 oz) self-raising flour

Frosting

75 g (3 oz) unsalted butter, softened
175 g (6 oz) icing sugar
2 tbsp strong black coffee

To decorate

Chocolate coffee beans or other small chocolate dragées
Demerara sugar

1 To make the cupcakes, preheat the oven to 180°C/350°F/gas mark 4. Line mini muffin trays with paper cases.

2 Melt the chocolate with the coffee granules or powder in a bowl set over a pan of hot water, stirring until smooth.

3 In a mixing bowl, beat the butter and muscovado sugar together until creamy. Gradually beat in the eggs, beating well after each addition. Stir in the flour and melted chocolate.

4 Spoon into the paper cases and bake for 12–15 minutes or until a skewer pushed into the centre of one of the cakes comes out clean. Cool in the trays for 10 minutes before removing to a wire rack to cool completely.

5 To make the frosting, beat the butter until creamy. Gradually sieve in the icing sugar, beating well after each addition, and then stir in the coffee.

6 Spread the frosting over the cupcakes and decorate with chocolate coffee beans and a light sprinkling of demerara sugar.

 *Tip*

If making these to serve with after dinner coffee, a coffee liqueur such as Tia Maria or Kahlúa can be added to the frosting instead of black coffee.

109

Sweetie treat

The ultimate birthday cake for any child and one that quite a few grown ups would appreciate as well! You'll need a special 2.4 litre (4¼ pt) giant cupcake tin to make it (pictured on page 7), which can be bought from cook shops or by mail order on the web.

Preparation time: 45 minutes
(plus cooling and decorating)
Cooking time: 1 hour 5 minutes–
1 ¼ hours
Serves: 12–14

Giant cupcake

275 g (10 oz) unsalted butter, softened
275 g (10 oz) golden caster sugar
Grated zest 1 lemon
6 large eggs, beaten
400 g (14 oz) self-raising flour
140 g (5 oz) plain flour
75 ml (3 fl oz) milk

Buttercream

115 g (4 oz) unsalted butter, softened
225 g (8 oz) icing sugar
2 tbsp lemon juice
3 tbsp seedless raspberry jam

To decorate

Small sweets, filled chocolate bars
cut into thin slices
White and milk chocolate writing icing

1 To make the cake, preheat the oven to 170ºC/325ºF/gas mark 3. Brush the two halves of a 2.4 litre (4¼ pint) giant cupcake tin with oil and dust with flour.

2 In a large mixing bowl, beat the butter, sugar and lemon zest together until creamy. Gradually beat in the eggs a little at a time, beating well after each addition. Sieve in the self-raising and plain flours and stir in with the milk.

3 Spoon the mixture into the tin, filling each half about three-quarters full and hollowing out the centres a little as both cakes will rise quite a lot. Bake for 1 hour 5 minutes–1¼ hours or until a skewer pushed into the centre of each cake comes out clean.

4 Cool in the tin for about 15 minutes before turning the cakes out on to a wire rack to cool completely.

5 To make the butter cream, beat the butter until creamy. Gradually sieve in the icing sugar, beating well after each addition, and stir in the lemon juice.

6 Trim the tops of the two cakes level and spread the base with the jam and about two-thirds of the butter cream. Sandwich the cakes together and spread the top part with the rest of the butter cream. Cover with small sweets and sliced chocolate bars pressing them gently into the butter cream to fix in place. Finally drizzle chocolate writing icing over the top.

 Tip

It's important to grease and flour the two halves of the tin well or the baked cakes will be difficult to turn out. Alternatively use a product such as Cake Release, available from cook shops, to make the task easier.

Fruit extravaganza

During the Christmas season when there is less choice of fresh berries and currants, top the cake with dried fruits and nuts and brush with warmed apricot jam to make them glisten. The cake doesn't require a special giant cupcake tin, it can be baked in a shallow heatproof basin, kugelhopf mould or other tin with sloping sides that has a capacity of about 1.4 litres (2½ pt).

Preparation time: 30 minutes (plus cooling)
Cooking time: about 1¼ hours
Serves: 10–12

Giant cupcake

175 g (6 oz) unsalted butter, softened
175 g (6 oz) light muscovado sugar
3 large eggs, beaten
115 g (4 oz) wholemeal self-raising flour
50 g (2 oz) plain flour
25 g (1 oz) cocoa powder
75 ml (3 fl oz) milk

To decorate

300 ml (½ pt) double cream
2 tbsp caster sugar
1 tsp vanilla essence
Fresh berries and currants such as strawberries, raspberries, blueberries, blackberries, redcurrants, blackcurrants, Cape gooseberries, grapes

1 To make the cake, preheat the oven to 170°C/325°F/gas mark 3. Brush a 1.4 litre (2½ pt) kugelhopf mould or similar with oil and dust with flour.

2 Beat the butter and light muscovado sugar together until creamy and then gradually mix in the eggs, beating well after each addition. Sieve together the wholemeal self-raising, plain flour and cocoa powder and stir in until evenly combined. Finally stir in the milk.

3 Spoon into the tin, hollow out the centre a little and bake for 1¼ hours or until a skewer pushed into the centre of the cake comes out clean. Cool in the tin for 15 minutes before turning out on to a wire rack to cool completely.

4 To decorate, whip the cream with the caster sugar and vanilla essence until holding its shape. Trim the top of the cake level and spread with half the cream. Pile on lots of different fresh berries, currants and other fruits.

5 Spoon the remaining cream into a piping bag fitted with a large star nozzle and pipe a collar of cream around the top of the cake. Keep refrigerated until ready to serve.

 *Tip*

A mix of self-raising and plain flours are used to give a firmer texture, similar to a Madeira cake, as this will provide a more solid base to support the fruit.

Not so guilty

Gooseberry streusel

The sharp tang of the gooseberries provides the perfect contrast to the sweet cupcakes with their crunchy topping. As gooseberries freeze well, these can be made all year round – defrost the gooseberries first before adding them to the cake mix.

Preparation time: 25 minutes (plus cooling)

Cooking time: 25 minutes

Makes: 12

Topping

50 g (2 oz) unsalted butter

50 g (2 oz) plain flour

50 g (2 oz) granola

1 tbsp golden caster sugar

Cupcakes

200 g (7 oz) fresh gooseberries, green or pink

175 g (6 oz) self-raising flour

115 g (4 oz) unsalted butter, softened

115 g (4 oz) golden caster sugar

2 large eggs

½ tsp vanilla essence

1 tbsp milk

Icing sugar, to dust

1 To make the topping, cut the butter into small pieces and rub it into the plain flour until like coarse breadcrumbs. Stir in the granola and sugar. Set aside whilst preparing the cake mix.

2 To make the cupcakes, top and tail the gooseberries, rinse, pat dry and halve or quarter according to size. Dust with a little of the flour.

3 Preheat the oven to 180°C/350°F/gas mark 4. Line a 12-cup muffin tray with paper cases.

4 Beat the butter and sugar together until creamy. Beat the eggs with the vanilla and gradually beat into the creamed mixture. Fold in the remaining flour, the gooseberries and milk.

5 Spoon the mixture into the cases and top with the granola mixture, pressing it down lightly with the back of the spoon or your fingers.

6 Bake for 25 minutes or until a skewer pushed into the centre of one of the cakes comes out clean. Cool in the tin for 10 minutes before removing to a wire rack to cool completely. Serve cold dusted with icing sugar.

 *Tip*

When gooseberries are out of season, replace them with 1 medium sized orange, peeled, segmented and chopped, and use the juice that runs out of the orange instead of the milk.

Beetroot and bitter chocolate

No, you're not seeing things, these cupcakes really are made with beetroot and its slightly sweet flavour complements the dark chocolate so well that even confirmed beetroot-phobes will be won over. If buying ready-cooked beetroot, make sure you look for plain beetroot and not slices or whole beets pickled in vinegar.

Preparation time: 30 minutes
(plus cooling and standing)
Cooking time: 20 minutes
Makes: 10

Cupcakes

175 g (6 oz) self-raising flour
1 tbsp cocoa powder
1 tsp baking powder
75 g (3 oz) dark chocolate with
at least 70% cocoa solids
75 g (3 oz) unsalted butter
175 g (6 oz) dark muscovado sugar
2 large eggs
175 g (6 oz) cooked beetroot, grated or
chopped to a coarse purée

Chocolate frosting

75 g (3 oz) icing sugar
25 g (1 oz) cocoa powder
40 g (1½ oz) unsalted butter
50 g (2 oz) dark muscovado sugar
Chocolate curls, to decorate

1 To make the cupcakes, preheat the oven to 180°C/350°F/gas mark 4. Line a muffin tray with 10 paper cases.

2 Sieve together the flour, cocoa and baking powder. Break up the chocolate into small pieces and place in a large bowl over a pan of simmering water. Cut up the butter and add to the chocolate with the sugar. Leave until the chocolate, butter and sugar have melted, stirring occasionally until smooth.

3 Remove the bowl to the work surface and let the melted chocolate mixture cool for a few minutes before beating in the eggs one at a time. Fold in the flour mixture and finally the beetroot.

4 Spoon into the paper cases and bake for 20 minutes or until just springy to the touch. Cool in the tin for 10 minutes before removing the cupcakes to a wire rack to cool completely.

5 To make the frosting, sieve the icing sugar and cocoa powder into a bowl. Cut up the butter into pieces and put in a small saucepan with the muscovado sugar and 2 tablespoons water. Heat gently until the butter and sugar melt, bring just to the boil, then remove from the heat and pour on to the icing sugar and cocoa. Whisk until smooth and then set aside to cool, stirring occasionally, until the frosting is thick enough to spread over the cupcakes. Decorate with chocolate curls.

Apple and prune cupcakes

These can be eaten plain or taken out of their paper cases whilst still warm and topped with a spoonful of thick natural yoghurt, mascarpone or vanilla ice cream.

Preparation time: 20 minutes
Cooking time: 20-25 minutes
Makes: 18 (using medium-size cases)

Cupcakes

225 g (8 oz) plain flour
2 tsp baking powder
115 g (4 oz) unsalted butter
115 g (4 oz) light muscovado sugar
2 dessert apples, total weight about 225 g (8 oz), cored and finely diced
75 g (3 oz) pitted prunes, chopped
1 large egg, beaten
100 ml (3½ fl oz) milk

Topping

1 dessert apple, cored and finely diced
25 g (1 oz) butter, melted
1 tsp ground cinnamon
6 sugar cubes, broken up into small pieces

1 Preheat the oven to 180°C/350°F/gas mark 4. Line muffin trays with 18 paper cases.

2 Sieve the flour and baking powder into a mixing bowl. Cut up the butter into small pieces and rub into the flour until the mixture resembles coarse breadcrumbs. Stir in the muscovado sugar, chopped apples and prunes. Beat together the egg and milk and stir in until evenly mixed. Spoon into the paper cases.

3 To make the topping, stir the chopped apple into the melted butter with the cinnamon and spoon on top of the cupcakes, pressing down gently with the back of the spoon. Scatter over the sugar pieces and bake for 20–25 minutes or until a skewer pressed into the centre of one of the cakes comes out clean. Cool in the tin for 10 minutes before removing to a wire rack. Eat warm or cold.

 *Tip*

Choose a tart, crisp variety of apple such as Granny Smith or Cox for the best texture and flavour and peel the apples or leave their skin on as preferred.

120

Carrot, orange and cinnamon

Sweeter and more indulgent than plain carrot cake or muffins, these make the perfect mid-morning pick-me-up when enjoyed with a reviving cappuccino.

Preparation time: 30 minutes (plus cooling)
Cooking time: 25–30 minutes
Makes: 12

Cupcakes

160 ml (5½ fl oz) sunflower oil
175 g (6 oz) light muscovado sugar
2 large eggs
Finely grated rind of 1 orange
175 g (6o z) self-raising flour
1 tsp ground cinnamon
75 g (3 oz) chopped walnuts
50 g (2 oz) raisins
200 g (7 oz) grated carrots

Cream cheese frosting

75 g (3 oz) cream cheese
25 g (1 oz) butter, softened
200 g (7 oz) icing sugar
2 tbsp chopped walnuts
Ground cinnamon, to dust

1 To make the cupcakes, preheat the oven to 180°C/350°F/gas mark 4. Line a 12-cup muffin tray with paper cases.

2 In a bowl whisk together the oil, sugar, eggs and orange rind until evenly combined. Sieve the flour and cinnamon into a separate bowl.

3 Stir the egg mixture into the dry ingredients and add the walnuts, raisins and carrots, mixing well.

4 Spoon the mixture into the cases and bake for 25–30 minutes or until just firm to the touch. Leave to cool in the tray for 10 minutes before transferring to a wire rack to cool completely.

5 To make the frosting, whisk together the cream cheese, butter and icing sugar until smooth and creamy.

6 Spread the frosting over the cupcakes, sprinkle with the chopped walnuts and dust lightly with cinnamon.

Niobrara County Library
Lusk, Wyoming 82225

 Tip

The cupcakes are cooked when they feel firm to the touch but are still slightly moist inside.

Malted raisin, oat and pecan

Malted milk powder was developed in Chicago and first became popular during the 1920s when it was added to milk shakes. Its naturally sweet flavour of malted barley makes it popular with children and adults alike.

Preparation time: 20 minutes
Cooking time: 20–25 minutes
Makes: 12

Cupcakes

140 g (5 oz) plain flour
50 g (2 oz) malted milk powder
2 tsp baking powder
100 g (3½ oz) oatmeal
50 g (2 oz) pecans, chopped
50 g (2 oz) raisins
175 g (6 oz) unsalted butter, softened
175 g (6 oz) light muscovado sugar
2 large eggs, beaten
2–3 tbsp milk

To decorate

200 g (7 oz) chocolate and hazelnut spread
Chocolate malted sweets
Cocoa powder, to dust

1 Preheat the oven to 180°C/350°F/gas mark 4. Line a 12-cup muffin tray with paper cases.

2 Sieve together the plain flour, malted milk powder and baking powder and stir in the oatmeal, pecans and raisins.

3 Beat the butter and sugar together until creamy. Beat in the eggs a little at a time until evenly combined and then fold in the dry ingredients and enough milk to make a soft mixture.

4 Spoon the mixture into the paper cases. As the mixture is quite heavy the cupcakes will not rise as much as lighter mixtures so the paper cases can be three-quarters full. Bake for 20–25 minutes until a skewer pushed into the centre of one of the cakes comes out clean. Cool in the tray for 10 minutes before transferring to a wire rack to cool completely.

5 Spread the tops of the cupcakes with the chocolate and hazelnut spread, top with chocolate malted sweets and dust lightly with cocoa powder.

 Tip

Make sure you buy malted milk powder rather than a packet of one of the instant malted drinks available, which may be displayed alongside.

Wheatgerm, banana and honey

Each grain of wheat contains a tiny golden germ that is a powerhouse of good things like vitamin E, folic acid, minerals and essential fatty acids. Wheatgerm is also an excellent source of fibre, making these cupcakes a real feel-good treat.

Preparation time: 20 minutes
Cooking time: 25 minutes
Makes: 15

Cupcakes

115 g (4 oz) unsalted butter, softened

225 g (8 oz) demerara sugar

2 tbsp clear honey

1 tsp ground ginger

140 g (5 oz) natural yoghurt

4 small ripe bananas (about 350 g / 12 oz unpeeled weight), peeled and chopped

2 large eggs

1 tsp almond essence

400 g (14 oz) self-raising flour

3 tbsp wheatgerm

40 g (1½ oz) chopped hazelnuts

1 Preheat the oven to 180°C/350°F/gas mark 4. Line muffin trays with 15 paper cases.

2 Cream the butter and 200 g (7 oz) of the sugar together, beating the butter first and then gradually beating in the sugar. Stir in the honey and ginger.

3 Liquidise the yoghurt, bananas, eggs and almond essence together until smooth. Mix together the flour and 2 tablespoons of the wheatgerm.

4 Add small amounts of the yoghurt mix to the creamed butter, alternately with the flour, stirring until evenly combined.

5 Spoon the mixture into the paper cases. Mix together the remaining sugar, wheatgerm and the chopped hazelnuts and sprinkle on top. Bake for about 25 minutes or a skewer pushed into the centre of one of the cakes comes out clean.

6 Cool in the tin for 10 minutes before removing to a wire rack. Eat warm or cold.

 *Tip*

If you don't have a liquidiser, mash the bananas with a fork and mix with the eggs before stirring or whisking into the beaten eggs.

Sweet potato and orange

Sweet potato cake is a favourite in America's Deep South where every cook has their own special variation. A cream cheese frosting such as the one used for the Carrot, orange and cinnamon cupcakes (see page 123) could replace the orange drizzle glaze if you prefer.

Preparation time: 20 minutes
Cooking time: 20 minutes
Makes: 16

Cupcakes

175 g (6 oz) unsalted butter, softened

140 g (5 oz) light muscovado sugar

Finely grated rind of 1 small orange

2 large eggs, beaten

225 g (8 oz) self-raising flour

225 g (8 oz) cooked sweet potato, mashed (about 2 medium-sized sweet potatoes)

4 tbsp natural yoghurt

1 tsp ground cinnamon

2 tbsp milk

To decorate

75 g (3 oz) caster sugar

Juice of 1 small orange

Orange segments and fine strips of rind, to decorate

1 Preheat the oven to 180°C/350°F/gas mark 4. Line muffin trays with 16 paper cases.

2 Beat the butter, muscovado sugar and orange rind together until creamy. Mix in the eggs a little at a time, beating between each addition, and adding a little flour if the mixture looks like curdling

3 Stir in the sweet potato and yoghurt followed by the remaining flour, the cinnamon and milk, mixing well. Spoon into the paper cases and bake for 20 minutes or until a skewer pushed into the centre of one of the cakes comes out clean.

4 Leave in the tray whilst you mix together the caster sugar and orange juice. Spoon this over the cupcakes while they are still warm and top with orange segments and fine strips of rind. When cool enough to handle, lift the cupcakes out of the tray and eat warm.

 Tip

The cupcakes can also be eaten cold but brush the orange segments with warm apricot jam or orange jelly marmalade to stop them drying out.

Plum, polenta and walnut

Although polenta is often dismissed as a rather bland accompaniment to Italian meat or fish dishes, it works well in a cake mixture, adding both flavour and an interesting texture that is slightly coarser than a normal sponge.

Preparation time: 25 minutes
Cooking time: 15–20 minutes
Makes: 12

Cupcakes

1 tbsp demerara sugar

50 g (2 oz) walnuts, chopped

175 g (6 oz) unsalted butter, softened

175 g (6 oz) golden caster sugar

Finely grated rind of 1 lemon

115 g (4 oz) polenta

3 large eggs, beaten

2 ripe but fairly firm plums, stones removed and chopped (unprepared weight about 140 g / 5oz)

160 g (5½ oz) plain flour

1½ tsp baking powder

Icing sugar tinted with a little powdered pink food colouring, to dust

1 Preheat the oven to 180°C/350°F/gas mark 4. Line a 12-cup muffin tray with paper cases.

2 Mix together the demerara sugar and walnuts and set aside. Beat the butter, caster sugar and lemon zest together until creamy and then stir in the polenta.

3 Beat in the eggs a little at a time. Dust the plums with a little of the flour. Stir in the rest of the flour and the baking powder. Finally mix in the plums until evenly combined.

4 Spoon the mixture into the paper cases and sprinkle over the demerara sugar and walnuts. Bake for 15–20 minutes until a skewer pushed into the centre of one of the cakes comes out clean. Cool for 10 minutes in the tin before transferring to a wire rack. Dust with pale pink icing sugar and eat warm or cold.

 *Tip*

The plums could be replaced with a peach, two apricots or three greengages, stoned and chopped, if preferred.

Free from...

Dairy free pear and almond

Based on a French frangipane mixture, these light cupcakes have a surprise orange filling and a sweet pear topping. Serve them warm fresh from the oven.

Preparation time: 25 minutes
Cooking time: 15–20 minutes
Makes: 10

Dairy free cupcakes

175 g (6 oz) ground almonds
100 g (3½ oz) caster sugar
1 tsp grated orange rind
3 large eggs, beaten
75 ml (3 fl oz) sunflower oil
100 g (3½ oz) self-raising flour
5 tbsp orange juice
8 tbsp orange jelly marmalade
5 pear halves
2 tbsp finely chopped pistachios

1 Preheat the oven to 180°C/350°F/gas mark 4. Line a muffin tray with 10 paper cases.

2 Put the almonds, sugar, orange rind, eggs, oil, flour and orange juice into a large mixing bowl and whisk or beat together until smooth.

3 Spoon half the mixture into the paper cases, top each with 1 teaspoon orange jelly marmalade and then add the rest of the mixture. Cut the pear halves into thin slices and lift a few on to the top of each cupcake, pressing down lightly so the slices fan out.

4 Bake for 15–20 minutes or until golden brown and firm to the touch. Warm the remaining marmalade and brush over the top of each cupcake. Sprinkle over the chopped pistachios and serve warm.

 *Tip*

Apples, peaches, nectarines or plums could be used instead of pears.

Egg free coconut and chocolate

A recipe that doesn't look as though it should work but it does beautifully to produce sweet, moist cakes that keep well in an airtight tin. They can also be frozen undecorated for up to 2 months.

Preparation time: 25 minutes (plus cooling)
Cooking time: 15-20 minutes
Makes 10

Egg free cupcakes
25 g (1 oz) cocoa powder
200 g (7 oz) self-raising flour
½ tsp baking powder
115 g (4 oz) golden caster sugar
325 ml (11 fl oz) full fat coconut milk
100 ml (4 fl oz) sunflower oil

Frosting
115 g (4 oz) icing sugar
1 tbsp cocoa powder
1–2 tbsp orange juice
2 tbsp desiccated coconut

1 To make the cupcakes, preheat the oven to 180°C/350°F/gas mark 4. Line a muffin tray with 10 paper cases.

2 Sieve the cocoa powder, flour and baking powder into a large jug and stir in the sugar. Add the coconut milk and sunflower oil and whisk everything together to make a smooth batter.

3 Carefully pour the mixture into the paper cases and bake for 15–20 minutes or until risen and a skewer comes out clean when pushed into the centre of a cake. Cool in the tin for 10 minutes, then remove to a wire rack to cool completely.

4 To make the frosting, sieve the icing sugar and cocoa powder into a bowl and stir in enough orange juice to make a smooth, spreadable icing. Spread the icing over the cupcakes and sprinkle the top of each one with desiccated coconut.

 **Tip**

Tinned coconut milk can separate on standing so give the can a good shake before you open it.

Fat free green tea and sultana

Although all cupcakes can be baked in silicone moulds instead of paper cases if you prefer, it's essential that silicone or non-stick paper cases are used for these or the baked mixture will stick like glue and the cupcakes be impossible to remove without leaving half the sponge behind – which would be a pity as these are moist and delicious.

Preparation time: 25 minutes (plus standing and cooling)
Cooking time: 12–15 minutes
Makes: 16 (using medium-size silicone cases)

Fat free cupcakes

1 green tea bag
140 g (5 oz) sultanas
115 g (4 oz) pitted soft dates, chopped
140 g (5 oz) dark muscovado sugar
2 large eggs, beaten
225 g (8 oz) wholemeal self-raising flour
1 tsp ground cinnamon or ginger

Green tea icing

250 g (9 oz) fondant icing sugar, sieved
3–4 tbsp green tea, hot or cold
2 tbsp each sultanas and chopped dates
Ground cinnamon or ginger, to dust

1 To make the cupcakes, put the tea bag in a large measuring jug and add 300 ml (½ pt) plus 3–4 tablespoons of hot, but not-quite-boiling, water. Set aside for 10 minutes, then remove the bag and pour 300 ml (½ pt) of the tea into a mixing bowl (the remaining 3–4 tablespoons is for the icing). Stir in the sultanas, dates and sugar. Leave to cool.

2 Preheat the oven to 180°C/350°F/gas mark 4. Beat the eggs into the tea mixture in the bowl and stir in the flour and cinnamon or ginger until evenly combined.

3 Set the silicone cases on a baking sheet and spoon the mixture into them. Bake for 12–15 minutes or until a skewer pushed into the centre of a cake comes out clean. Leave to cool completely before icing.

4 To make the icing, sieve the icing sugar into a bowl and stir in enough of the reserved green tea to make a spreadable icing. Coat the tops of the cupcakes with the icing and decorate with a few sultanas and chopped dates. Dust with a little ground cinnamon or ginger.

 *Tip*

As the cake batter is quite heavy it won't rise a great deal so the silicone cases can be filled almost to the top.

Sugar free parsnip and pecan

The natural sweetness of parsnips, dried fruit and pressed apple juice make these delicious cupcakes a treat not just for those needing to follow a sucrose-free diet but for anyone who finds ordinary cupcakes with their creamy frostings too sweet. If extra sweetness is required, add a little fructose or one of the commercial sweeteners that are suitable for diabetics.

Preparation time: 20 minutes
Cooking time: 15-20 minutes
Makes: 15

Sugar free cupcakes

2 large eggs
150 ml (¼ pt) sunflower oil
250 g (9 oz) wholemeal self-raising flour
1 tsp baking powder
1 tsp ground mixed spice
225 g (8 oz) raw parsnips, finely grated
75 g (3 oz) sultanas
75 g (3 oz) dried figs, chopped
200 ml (7 fl oz) unsweetened apple juice
15 pecan halves

1 Preheat the oven to 180°C/350°F/gas mark 4. Line muffin trays with 15 paper cases.

2 Put the eggs in a mixing bowl and whisk in the oil in a thin stream so it combines smoothly with the eggs. Stir or whisk in the flour, baking powder and mixed spice, add the parsnips, sultanas and figs and mix until everything is combined. Finally stir in the apple juice.

3 Spoon the mixture into the paper cases and press a pecan half on top of each. Bake for 15–20 minutes or until a skewer pushed into the centre of a cake comes out clean.

4 Cool in the trays for 10 minutes before removing to a wire rack. Eat warm or cold.

Niobrara County Library
Lusk, Wyoming 82221

 Tip

Instead of parsnips, the cakes can also be made with the same quantity of grated raw carrots.

Index

Suppliers

Equipment for making cupcakes such as bun and muffin trays, silicone moulds, paper cases and edible decorations can be purchased from:

Lakeland
Tel: 015394 88200
www.lakeland.co.uk

Cake Craft Shop
Tel: 01732 463 573
email: info@cakecraftshop.co.uk
www.cakecraftshop.co.uk

As well as kitchen shops and larger supermarkets and department stores.

The giant cupcake tin used on page 110 is available from Lakeland.